OMG...I Can Do It!

Verses Kindler Publication

Verses Kindler Publication.

Website: www.verseskindlerpublication.com

OMG... I Can Do It

By: Mr. Vikas Goel

ISBN: 978-93-5605-600-8

NON-FICTION STORIES 1st Edition

Price: INR 299 / $15

Disclaimer

OMG... I Can Do It is written by Vikas Goel.

The published work is the original contents of the author and he has done his best to edit and make it plagiarism-free.

The characters may be fictitious or based on real events but they are not meant to hurt anyone's feelings nor portray anything against any caste or system. Any resemblance of names of actual person, place or institute is purely coincidental to carry forward the story.

In case of any plagiarized write-up, the author is solely responsible for it, the publisher would not be responsible for it.

Preface

Hi, I'm Vikas- the quintessential backbencher and the 'good for nothing' according to my teachers & peers.

Hi again, I'm Vikas- the CEO of 3 companies that have worked with Fortune 500 clients and made $15M in revenue so far and counting.

And before you wonder, let me clarify, this is one and the same person.

My intention here is to make this as unlike any typical motivational and inspirational story that you may have read as possible because, in reality, this is not just another success saga. I have been at both extremities of the pendulum of life. I've experienced the carefreeness that accompanies having no distinct goals to work towards. But, I've also lived through a transformational experience that opened my eyes to how my goals would dictate my life's course.

It taught me in the quickest, maybe harshest, and yet most effective way that I need to get up, get going, and keep going.

And that's exactly what I did.

Table of Contents

Chapter 1

"If you can't fly, then run. If you can't run, then walk. If you can't walk, then crawl, but whatever you do, you have to keep moving."

- Martin Luther King Jr.

Imagine a montage playing from a movie that showcases the initially directionless life of the teen hero. You would probably be visualizing scenes of leisurely days and stress-free nights. Every day felt like one moment after the other that simply ran on autopilot. There were no quests to conquer or no drive to excel in anything.

For the longest time, this felt enough for me because I had never had a glimpse of what the other side looked like. From where I was, the grass looked greener since I was content in my situation. Pulling myself out of this place of complacency was the most valuable and best gift I could give myself, and yes, this is counting all the luxury shoes, and cars, and foreign trips that I indeed treated myself to later in life.

Let's emphasize on that last part, 'later in life', because it is essential to clarify that I was not born with a silver spoon in my mouth. Everything that I indulged myself and my family with was hard-earned, and that made it exponentially sweeter.

My family comprised of my parents, my elder brother and sister, and me. We lived in a good locality of South Delhi. In my limited knowledge of the way the world works, my initial impression of our financial situation was over-optimistically good. I used to wander out of home and look at posh surroundings, fancy and high-rise buildings, impeccably dressed people, and a bustling hub of restaurants and shops. However, I slowly came to the realization that despite the glamour of everything around us, we were occupants of the category 'urban poor'.

The family that I have been blessed with shielded me from these realities for the longest time and I was well into my teenage years when I finally started seeing things for what they were. For the early years of my life, I had on rose-colored glasses.

I had loving parents who left no stone unturned in caring for me. I always did, and to date adore my father, yet my bond with my mother will always remain extra special. Every child has a superhero growing up; usually, they are fictitious characters who flit on and off screen, but I was lucky enough to have my superhero around me all the time.

She was the first, and real-life example I saw of what strength and resilience truly mean. She was the backbone of our household, and the foundation beneath our feet that kept our world stable. I saw the undying courage she showed while dealing with every situation that came her way, along with the positivity she radiated while doing so. She struggled a lot, and I'm sure there may have been times when she felt like crumbling, yet she held everything together for us. She was, and to date is the biggest source of inspiration for all of us.

Right from my childhood, the general consensus had been that I look like her. Relatives used to gushingly tell me how good it was for a son to have his mother's features and it used to make me very happy to have that in common with her. As the years went by, I started noticing to my utmost pleasure that my similarities with her went beyond physical appearances.

My deepest nature and personality too evolved to be like hers, and I would surely like this to be taken on record as a brag! I want to continue embodying all the good values I have seen in her, and I believe it's the guiding light that will take me upwards and onwards to better things.

My siblings too have been a key character in my life's plot.

At the very outset, my brother was like the one student in class that everyone slightly envied; he had his life and his priorities sorted out, and studying always occupied the prime position on his vision board. This naturally translated into exceptional grades, being adored by teachers and parents alike, and setting out expectations into the world that the same set of genetics can produce another such prodigy. But, along came me, and we were as unlike one another as chalk and cheese. My family took a little longer to see these glaring differences, and they once harbored dreams of me becoming a doctor. As I mentioned, I was willing to go with the flow and did not have any dream profession in mind. I used to hear my friends and classmates discuss how they wanted to enter the police force or fly rockets to space; such thoughts never penetrated my mind, and I was willing to silently go along with the scheme of events that life had prescribed for me.

When I turned this around and took charge of my fate, my brother transitioned into the role of a mentor and trusted advisor for me. He had my back through all the ups and downs, and he helped me from straying off the path. I largely owe my achievements to him, for he took a bet on me at a time when perhaps I would not have done the same for myself.

My sister was my biggest cheerleader and a companion who never left my side through all the twists and turns in the roller coaster of my life. She supported me in every way possible, be it financially when she selflessly spent parts of her salary toward my tuition, or emotionally when she helped me realize my potential and encouraged me to further pursue my education. Had it not been for her guidance and generosity, my path may have led elsewhere, and I shall remain indebted to her for steering me to the right destination.

My educational journey started out at an average school. We did not have the means to enroll in any premium institute, but my parents tried to secure the best future for us with the limited resources they had. My interest and overall enthusiasm for education can be gauged from the fact that some of the fondest memories I have of school are from when it used to finish every day.

I initially found it hard to adjust to being away from my mother and home for so many hours. In my nursery and kindergarten years, I used to wait eagerly for the last bell to ring which gave me the freedom to run out and meet my mother. She often used to take me to eat ice cream, and that sweet treat at the end made the entire day worth it.

Another fond memory of my schooling years is also based outside of the classroom. I used to religiously get together with a group of friends after school every day and we used to play cricket. That was a time and place where every child playing there just became one of a group and found a sense of belonging; I was no longer the low performer of the class and there was nobody who gave me an inferiority complex due to their good marks.

While we were playing, we were all just boys who wanted to have fun. I felt comfortable in my own skin there and accepted for exactly whom I was.

Sadly, the situation within the 4 walls of the classroom was slightly different. The traditional and typical mindset for a child to do well in school is either for him to be academically brilliant or socially adored. You had to either stand out in one of these aspects, or risk becoming a wallflower and be cast away into oblivion. Some people are blessed to instantaneously find their belonging in one category or the other, but I was not one of them. I was left hanging in the middle, barely getting by classes and struggling to secure a good place in the social order. Put two and two together, and you might have made an educated guess about how I did in school.

Spoiler alert, not too well.

When it came to studies, calling myself an average student too might be an overrepresentation. I was inherently disinterested whenever it came to learning and studying. The idea of mugging up things from a textbook, or memorizing bookish lessons that I saw no practical applications for never appealed to me. This was probably the case for a lot of students; but to make matters worse for myself, I never found the willingness that they did to just deal with it and try to do well in what was expected of me.

I went the opposite route and continued doing the mere basics that kept me safe from failing, but never let me excel. I didn't particularly like or enjoy any subject taught in school, but I had a special aversion to maths. Pretty ironic, considering numbers are such a major part of my life now, but back then I had no affinity or interest in them.

I was faring no better on the social side, and I mostly stuck with a small group of friends that I had luckily found. If I'm being brutally honest, I would think of them less as true friends and more as some people who had decided to take me under their wing. They gave me a place among them and let me be a part of the group, however, I always felt distinctly different from them. They belonged to the breed of class toppers, and I always felt an invisible barrier between me and them. Despite them never intentionally doing so, I had a self-imposed inhibition against gelling with them.

I believed that I was somehow lesser than them since I wasn't scoring as well. When discussions about future careers came up, it was an assumed fact that I would have nothing to contribute and hence my voice went unheard.

I was the underdog, and nobody shied away from making me feel like one. It was evident from their demeanor and interactions with me that they had taken it for granted that I would be nothing to look out for. I had been dismissed as a contender in the race of professional achievements; but now, they look at me in a very different light. I wish I had the confidence to hold my own ground among them back then as I do now, but I was under the mistaken assumption that their marks meant everything.

Today, however, they know and I know that it's far from the reality.

The teenage years are always a period of drastic change and evolution. We develop strong opinions, form concrete notions about ourselves and the world around us, and this time plays a pivotal role in how our lives shape up. I was faced with a major turning point shortly after becoming a teenager. I had slowly understood that our economic status did not place us on the highest rung of the ladder. I used to wonder why we did not have some of the luxuries that I used to hear about; I yearned to have an AC at home or a sleek car to travel by.

My first real eye-opening experience came when I desperately wanted to get a pair of Action Shoes, and I just could not ask for them. I realized that my parents would not be able to say it to my face, but the simple truth was that we could not afford it. It was scary to be exposed to such a harsh reality at that age, however, some good came of it too. It fired up a desire in me to change this situation, and that desire has been the driving force behind everything I have achieved to date. I resolved never to demand for materialistic things again.

I somehow matured overnight once this ball of realizing our financial limitations got rolling. I am today in a position to acknowledge that it was a blessing in disguise because it helped me turn my life around. This happened sometime during the 9th grade of school, and I ironically understood the importance of studies at the tail end of my schooling.

I knew I had to find a way out for myself and my family and attain a position in life that would give me every comfort that I needed. It struck me that education will always remain a lifeline that I can count on; it would give me the means to earn a good livelihood and provide for myself and my loved ones.

It was a typical case of 'better late than never'. Even if it was the last 2 years left in my school, I was motivated to do well and fight my way up to the top 35-40% of the class.

I was no longer willing to bow down and simply take things if and when they came my way. I wanted to get ahead, work hard, and take them for myself.

This phase was, simultaneously, the beginning and the end of a lot of things.

I bid goodbye to the boy that I had once been; the one who had no idea of what he wanted and thereby had no motivation to work toward anything. It was the birth of a new Vikas. I would not say that it was a dramatic, transformational moment that brought order to my life in a split second. It was a journey, a long yet highly rewarding process that changed the way I perceived myself and the world around me.

I feel pangs of regret over some of the things that I lost out on till I reinvented myself. I know I was failing to meet the rightful expectations that my parents and brother had of me back then. My teachers and friends too would have been largely disappointed, and I yearned for a chance to make it up to them.

I would love to do it all over again; take this new version of myself back to school and apply all the things I've learned over the years to give it a different outcome. There is nothing that fascinates me more than acquiring skills and knowledge now. I have a thirst for learning new concepts and opening my mind to new ideas, and I believe this would have been a game-changer for my schooling years.

However, I still stand by the thoughts of the child in me who failed to see the benefit of blindly mugging up things without practically understanding them. If I had the freedom in school to learn things that can be applied in real life and with which I can enrich my life or of those around me, I too would be the typical class topper.

From being a young boy who struggled with finding the right words to express myself, I am now someone who can make people interested in hearing me talk. I can command their interest, and I think the biggest source of this change was the self-assurance that I built up over the years. I had it fixed in my mind that I could not communicate well, and hence I stayed in that cocoon.

However, picking up the pebbles of the small wins that I earned along the way taught me that I can stack those up to create a path up to the highest victories. Every win, however minor or trivial it may seem, contributes to the big wins.

There's an interesting thought that challenged me and inspired me through every phase of life. I could articulate it only later, but the essence has always remained with me and helped me make some good, sound decisions.

Is it really apt to say that one needs confidence to try to do something? Or is it that confidence will come to you only after you take the plunge and do it anyway?

I discovered and unleashed my complete strength only after taking actions to realize it. Hence, my personal experience has taught me that the latter holds true, and this is the mantra I've applied to keep forging a bright path ahead for myself.

Chapter 2

"The best part of being an underdog is that the only direction you can move is upwards."

- *Source Unknown*

It is a popular phrase that 'Life and Time are the best teachers'. Allow me to give this my own spin, wherein I say that they are indeed the most impactful and effective teachers.

And I'll elaborate on my reasons for rewording this age-old saying that has been passed down for generations.

When we hear the term 'the best teacher', our mind naturally gravitates to a school, college, or tuition teacher; someone with a calming temperament, and abundant patience, who cleared confusing concepts and perhaps helped you do well in an exam that you had been dreading.

Having learned some very significant and crucial lessons at the hands of life and time, let me tell you that none of these have any qualities that you imagined for 'the best teacher'.

They are relentless when they throw out challenges at you, and never wait till you catch up before moving on in their own decided path. They never allow you the luxury of patience, and you simply must grasp things at the momentum and pace that they're trying to teach you.

But, when you think of a teacher in terms of the impact they had on your life, or how effectively they taught you, your defining criteria automatically change. They might not be your favorite, or have been kind, fun-loving, or patient. But you always remember them through the lessons they taught you and will be grateful for them. Such was my journey of learning from life and time, which led me to coin a new term for them.

The realization of what my family's true financial situation was, and the shedding of the illusion they had created so as to not worry or trouble me, changed something in me forever.

I wish I could say my transformation was instant, like in the movies. Captain America, my favorite superhero, had a magical version 2.0 transformation, but I also admired his original self—resilient and unwavering despite obstacles. My transformation was slower, driven by a desire to excel in studies and secure a better future for myself and my family, who had always supported me.

A fierce determination burned within me, but self-doubt lingered. I felt like I was in a one-sided competition with my brother, an academic genius and the family's pride. In reality, he never saw it that way and was always supportive and encouraging. Yet, I feared falling short and tarnishing the legacy he had built. It was my own imagination creating this pressure, making me anxious about the journey I had chosen. My brother's golden-hearted nature only amplified my resolve to succeed, not just for myself, but for him and the family who believed in me.

It took me a while, but I eventually decided to make these fears into my strengths. I reasoned that the very worst outcome of my efforts would be that I would have remained at the position where I was. This was a small price to pay considering what was at stake, and paled in comparison with the umpteen positive results that I could perhaps bring forth.

Hence, I made up my mind and started my transformational journey.

Like a tortoise who was in it for the long run to win the race, I took baby steps of progress. I tried to lengthen my attention span, absorb myself more in the words of my textbooks, assimilate, and recollect the lessons.

The other subjects were more respectful and responsive to my fervent attempts, but not mathematics. It remained stubborn, unhelpful, and unyielding. I'm making an educated guess to assume that for a lot of you, math was the monster that terrorized your student days.

I was in the very same boat; and despite the rough undercurrents of disappointment that the subject brought my way, I kept steering ahead. Armed with the slight improvements in my academic acumen and the vast improvements in my mindset, I sat for the pre-board examinations. In a scene straight from my worst nightmare, with special effects of shame and tension, the results showed that I had failed in mathematics.

Till that point, I had thought that though math was a beast putting up a tough fight, I would be able to scrape through unharmed and dodge its fierce attacks. However, seeing that paper with the glaring red marks all over and the score that was below the passing line made me realize just how dangerous my opponent was.

I had merely 20 days left for the final board exams and this came as an eye-opening jolt. To add insult to injury, my math teacher asked to speak with my mother. He had taught my brother too, and he wasted no opportunity in showcasing and making me realize how apart us two brothers were.

He explained to my mother how, in his opinion, my performance was not suitable to even get across the passing threshold for the main exam. He recommended that I should file for an alternative set of exams and skip giving the board paper altogether.

Now, if you're thinking that this other exam was meant for students like me who refused to be tied down by the strict binds of curriculum and were instead fairly tested on practical life skills and knowledge, you're unfortunately very wrong in the assumption. I wish there were an exam like that, so that no student would have to face the extreme pressure that I did.

The reality of the exam that my teacher had suggested was starkly different. It was not something that embraced the differences between students and tested them in the areas that truly mattered. It was more like a physical kind of exam to just get a student to pass.

The subtext, which was never said but was clearly implied, was that the exam was the last resort for lost causes. And in the eyes of my teacher, I was one such lost cause.

Fast forward to many years later where my achievements and the trajectory of my life are a testament that I was not what everyone perceived me to be. Consistently high scores, acing every project or homework, or being a model student were things that were falsely fixed in the mind of society at large as the only signs for someone to do well in life.

I too was swept up by this brainwashing, and I had resigned to my fate that the topper batchmates were the only ones with the potential to make something of themselves. Because my peers and teachers never even let me visualize myself at their level, I underestimated my potential that I would, one day, surpass it.

This calls for certain clarification. I don't mean to imply that I've done better than others, or make bold declarations of being more successful. All I mean is that I excelled in the field I chose for myself despite not being the typical front-bencher and overachieving student. And the crux of the matter here is that the atmosphere around me at the time was not conducive to students like me holding out this hope.

I dearly hope that has changed now, and that my story resonates with anyone who feels or has felt this way at any point of time.

I learned this over time, and so I'd like to share a quick dose of wisdom here for the benefit of others. Studies, or academic brilliance is not everything in life. What matters is finding your passion, sticking with it, and working toward it.

Instead of chasing high scores, I eventually learned that street-smart thinking, survival tactics, and networking skills would be the companions that would accompany me on my walk to success. I am eternally glad that I found the courage and wisdom to deviate from the traditional paths set in stone for us, and pursue contentment in my profession.

In my characteristic style, I realize I've deviated a bit in my storytelling too. I realize I've given away most of the ending, without recounting the instances leading up to it.

Circling back to the shockwaves I felt upon failing the pre-boards and the complete loss of faith of my teachers in me, they charged me up from within to change the course of my destiny.

The easiest option, to crumble and give up, was waiting for me to embrace it with open arms. But I turned my back on it and instead worked harder than I ever had till then.

I drilled down through the entire syllabus and question papers of past years to find 5-6 topics that were most likely to be included in the paper, and with which I could surely pass.

I had lost a few days in the aftermath of my poor performance in the pre-boards and in narrowing down what I needed to study. Thus, I was on a strict deadline of merely 10 days before I would be facing my old nemesis, mathematics, in the board exams. I created a plan for myself wherein I put in a rigorous 16-17 hours of studying daily.

I also joined a tuition class at that time, which is a very big thing for me to date. You may be wondering why this is so. The reason being that my sister worked at the coaching center where I took tuition, and part of her salary went toward the payment for it.

Despite being young herself, she took up the responsibility of getting me all the help I needed to do well in the exam. If not for myself, I knew I wanted to do well for her, and I slogged for it.

Working toward a goal so strictly felt empowering, but I knew I had no control over the results it would bring. Having put in my 100%, I went for the paper with the mantra 'que sera sera' chiming out in my mind.

A few weeks later, when the results were announced, I got a glimpse of what hard work and determination can materialize into. Against all odds, I had not only passed in the exam, but scored 78 marks; which was higher than I had ever expected from myself.

It was my first taste of success, and boy, was it sweet!

It made me realize that much like an untapped reservoir, I had a lot of power in me that I had never harnessed. Perhaps I needed to be pushed to my very limit to unleash it. In my own eyes and mind, I took a leap from just being an average somebody to someone who would make people think, *"He's got something in him!"*

I had started transforming the perception I had of myself, but it was still a work in progress and I was not quite there yet to take confident bets on myself. I was intrigued by the idea of taking science after 10th.

It was not the case that I was exceptionally good at any subject related to it, but I harboured a dream of perhaps taking it up and seeing where it led me. However, the shadows of doubt crept up and started whispering things to me that made me question my dream. *"Am I capable enough to do science?"* was the inhibition that kept clouding my mind.

The result? I convinced myself that the stream was not for me, and I turned to the direction of commerce and accounting instead.

The decision worked well in my favor. The subjects were reasonably interesting for me and easy to follow, and I cruised through the 11th grade. I was nowhere close, or frankly interested in becoming the golden boy of the classroom, but in a sharp contrast from what my early schooling days were like, I managed to perform fairly well throughout.

As I entered the 12th grade, 'board exams' became the buzz word once again that occupied everyone's mind. I needed to emerge from the bubble of comfort that I was in, since I knew that simply staying at the level that I was at might be enough for other times, but not when my future college was on the line. I needed to go a notch, or best-case scenario, several notches above in my scores to land a good college.

I had already bid goodbye to my days of frivolity and academic disinterest, and I ventured ahead to tackle this new challenge of my life too with the same resolve that I had earlier built. It helped me to a great extent and I ended up scoring 78% in the exams.

However, we Delhi-ites don't believe in settling for anything average and the colleges there are no different. My scores were relatively good, but not good enough to get my name on the roster of any good college in Delhi.

I did, however, gain admission into a tier 2-3 university in Dehradun to do my BBA. I was a little skeptical to take up this opportunity. Having never stayed away from home before, and lacking the inherent faith in myself that I could handle myself out in the world, I didn't know moving away would be the best step for me.

But my brother encouraged me to take what turned out to be one of the most rewarding experiences of my life. He went a step ahead from encouragement, and even financed my course. Like in many other instances over the course of my life, he nudged me back then toward making the right choice.

It was like I had been uprooted from my world and placed in a fantasy land. Everyone was alien to me, and everything felt different from what I knew. However, I gradually made my place there and learned some of the most valuable lessons that took me a long way.

I don't only mean academically, but the entire experience of living on my own, finding like-minded and good friends, and building my social and soft skills were the most delightful by-products of my education.

There is so much I have to recollect, share, and be grateful for about those times that it warrants separate attention of its own, which I will provide in due time.

In terms of academics, the journey was as smooth-sailing as I could hope for. I passed in every exam and graduated with a score of 62%. I wouldn't say it was the best work but I did my very best to get there. It was a stepping stone in my quest to reinvent myself and become someone whom I would be proud to look at in the mirror.

And today, that's what I am.

Chapter 3

"Life's a climb but the view is great."

- Miley Cyrus

Imagine you've seen a wonderful movie, one that soon turns out to be your favorite. If you ever decide to rewatch it, you will likely be most interested in the part where the story really picks up, or where the hero comes into his element, or there's the introduction of a dynamic new character.

If my life were a movie (and who knows, that might be the next step for me after this book!) the hostel experience during my BBA would be that part.

Interestingly, it is where all three of the points that I mentioned which make a particular scene stand out from the rest of the film happened in my real life. The story of my life picked pace and shifted in a great direction. I broke free from the cocoon I had built around myself, driven by the discouraging thoughts of not being good enough. And not just one, but I was blessed to have many new people enter my life and change it for the better.

Thus, while I'm walking you through scene by scene of my life through my words, those years deserve their due mention. It's also the part that I would love to recollect; immerse myself once again in those simple rooms that became a doorway to a new world for me, those tentative friendships initially forged with awkwardness and shyness but which became some of the most rewarding relationships of my life, and every conversation that felt easy and casual at the moment but which built up my personality and confidence in a way that I could have never foreseen.

The visionary behind this turning point, who somehow knew that it would help me so much even before it happened, was my brother. Had it not been for him, and the push he gave me at the right time, I would have stayed complacent in my city and home, and the comforts they offered. But, he advised me that comfort was not what I should be seeking, for it would never force me to go the extra mile and discover myself.

"Hostel will teach you to live like a man," he told me. And so, placing my faith like always in his wisdom and his love that wanted me to excel and do well for myself, I packed my bags and set off on a thrilling new journey.

I'd like to paint a picture of me here, walking along with a rucksack on my back, countless inhibitions in my mind, and no foreseeable target in sight. But the picture has two others by my side. Along with my immense faith in my brother's decision-making, it was these two companions who made the transition from home life to hostel life easier for me.

I have known Mayank for a long time, and I can say that it wasn't very hard to see why I connected with him at all. Growing up in Delhi, we found ourselves traversing parallel struggles—confused about our place in the world, eager to please our families, but unsure of the way to go about it. It felt like we were going on similar paths, carving out our future in each of our own ways while carrying with us the weight of expectations.

It was in this shared sense of uncertainty that we found common ground, and our friendship naturally took root. As we spent more time together, we realized that, despite the different routes we might take, we were both driven by the same goal: to make something meaningful of ourselves.

After the 12th board exams, he knew that engineering or accounting were out of his league and hence he turned towards BBA. I first met Ajay in a tuition class. The class surely helped me to a certain extent to boost my marks, but I would still say that the best outcome from it was the strong bond that I formed with Ajay.

He was my constant partner for studies, and somehow those sessions achieved what few other things could; they actually made me sit and focus for hours on end and learn things very efficiently. In one of these shared sessions, Ajay and I cooked up an idea. We imagined ourselves as future finance moguls and thought that we would both end up in that field. We also had an idea that we thought would help us uncover a jackpot of earnings; we wanted to open a pool parlor.

Looking back, we laugh about how crazy of a thought it was. But even if it didn't materialize, it gave me a ton of happy and fun memories of our planning phase. And who knows, perhaps that unfinished pool parlor venture was what sowed the seed of entrepreneurship in me that grew and thrived over the years.

We attempted the entrance exam for the college in Dehradun together, but neither of us was too serious about taking admission there, because we were holding out the belief that we would get selected in some college in or near Delhi. As the days passed, and we ran out of excuses to give ourselves for why we were not getting any more admission calls, it was time for us to make a decision.

My brother had already expressed his opinion about me taking up the seat I had got there. Mayank too had started thinking along the same lines, wherein he felt that though it would not be the dream college for any of us, but we could stay together and make it an enjoyable experience. And so, the three of us welcomed this new course that our lives were taking and set off.

The hostel itself was like a giant melting pot- like different metals are put into one to seamlessly blend together, students of different cultures, backgrounds, interests, and opinions were brought together to form one large community. Though we knew that we always would have the safety blanket of a fixed set of friends in these unfamiliar surroundings, Mayank, Ajay and I had decided to not stay limited to our group and try our best to mingle with the new crowd.

And while I can't speak for them, that decision was a game-changer for me.

During my earlier years, my social life was limited to only meeting and interacting with a fixed set of people. The maximum amount of time is usually spent with one's family, I was no different. In their way, my family imparted innumerable lessons to me. My mother taught me strength, my father taught me responsibility, my brother taught me resilience, and my sister taught me selflessness.

I tried to absorb whatever I could from them. However, I had slipped into a place of ultimate comfort and familiarity with them (as, of course, happens for everyone with respect to their family), and I was never pushed to challenge myself while interacting with them. I could say every unfiltered thought in my mind without worrying too much about its repercussions on my social acceptance, or I could just stay mum if I chose to without coming across as snobbish or reserved or uninformed.

But in hostel, where I did not have my people around me and instead had to make my place among a new crowd, it pushed me to become a better version of myself.

Over time, we formed a large group comprised of 16 or so boys. We named ourselves 'Strikers', for we thought it was a cool and trendy name; one that would be remembered by us and others for a long time. Unlike my group in school, I was truly a part of Strikers. And not just included for the sake of it, but I was a valued and well-liked member.

Building this group was my first real experience of networking and connecting with people, and I was surprised at how well I was faring in it. Till then, I had my reservations about striking conversations with people. *"What can I even say to people that they might find interesting?"* was the major fear that held me back. If I had perhaps put this nagging voice of doubt in my head on mute and actually taken the leap, I might have realized years before that I could engage easily with people.

A significant inhibition that I had back then was because of my language. At that time, I was not too fluent in English and I wrongfully thought it would always keep me tied down to the bottom rung of the social ladder. Even ordering a simple meal at McDonald's was a struggle for me because of my inherent lack of confidence in my speaking skills.

But those hostel years helped me learn a very important lesson; something that I think every young Vikas out there needs to know right from the start so that he may never feel the way I did, and would never make the mistake of hiding away like I did.

Language is nothing more than a tool. It is simply a medium used for communication; your thoughts and the essence behind them matter much more than the language or words that you use to put them across. If anyone judges you on the basis of your language, you can safely assume that person is not a valuable or positive influence in your life.

My college friends wholeheartedly accepted me, despite the self-doubts that would initially hold me back. They seemed to enjoy discussions with me even though my grammar and vocabulary were not always on point, and I came to the understanding that the worries about my lack of fluency in English were in my mind alone; they did not care about it half as much as I did. And this helped me reach the level of acceptance that I now have.

I trust myself enough to know that people will hear me out. The self-assurance this instilled in me almost made me feel like a different person altogether. And it only got reinforced and reaffirmed with every new phase of my life, till I have reached the point of passing on this wisdom to others in need. *"Just be yourself while interacting with people; English is not everything,"* is all that you must remember.

I also learned, to my utmost delight, that I had a rather convincing way of talking and people believed in me. I had not realized then how important this aspect would be for my career. In my line of work, trust in a man's word means a lot. I would have had to cultivate this trait sooner rather than later if I wanted to thrive in my business, but luckily for me, it was another advantageous outcome of living in a hostel.

Those years taught me how to coexist happily with people from all walks of life; how to share a common space and belongings, and how to have each other's backs, and tackle every calamity, however big it may be, together. And the most beautiful part of such relations is that when you stand to support 5 people, all those 5 will stand to support you. That spirit of unity makes you bond for life.

And lastly, it inculcated a strong sense of discipline and taught me the value of money. I did not even realize when I absorbed these big learnings; but they have stayed with me till date and when I now reflect back, I can correlate it to my hostel days.

I was used to the delicacies prepared lovingly for me by my mother. Being the youngest of the house, everyone's food choices were dictated as per my preferences. However, anyone who has been in a hostel can imagine what a rough shock I was in for. Not only was the food there very tasteless, but I had to eat whatever was made. I could not keep spending money to eat outside. And that's how I learned to make the best of any situation I was in, step out of my comfort zone, and as my brother had predicted, I truly started living like a man instead of a pampered and sheltered boy.

Hostel was, indeed, the most eye-opening phase of my life. I believe it taught me more than even the course or college did, and I would hail it as the best learning experience I've had.

Alongside that, the role and contributions of my friends and the other positive influences I met there cannot be emphasized enough.

Let me start with Mayank. When I said earlier that we came from similar backgrounds, it meant that he too had been conditioned with the thought that he possessed no extraordinary skills or abilities, or was not gifted in any unique way.

But Mayank's subtle yet impactful response to this situation was, *"So what?!"* He made up for the absence of any special skills through sheer hard work; and that, in my opinion, made him extraordinarily special. He helped me realize that hard work, which is in your control, can get you to a good place in life even without inbuilt talent, which anyway you have no control over.

Ajay, my would-be business partner, taught me a different kind of lesson. He was always very relaxed and the typical 'chill' young guy. He never stressed too much about things, and was content with wherever life took him.

He mostly remained happy with whatever he had, and his ambitions were a stark contrast to mine. I was on a mission to change my life, give everything I could to my family, and make a name for myself, but his goals in life were very different. While his attitude of never letting worries bring him down was undoubtedly a good thing to pick up from him, and was helpful in protecting me from undue pressure, seeing him also made me realize that I did not have the luxury of being like that.

I could not be that carefree or not work toward those strict goals I had set for myself; not when the financial security and comfort of my family was on the line.

A refreshingly new influence in my life was Sharad, a highly tech-savvy person whom I became close friends with. I looked up to him immensely, and he was always willing to extend a helping arm toward me.

I had never owned a computer of my own back then. I was quite comfortable with it and knew how to use it from the things we were taught in school, and from the rare times that I got my hands on it. But Sharad had his own and he was always kind enough to allow us all to use it, and went a step ahead to help us with it whenever he could. His generosity touched my heart, and left a lasting impact that made me want to be selfless and giving too. I hope I have been able to achieve that. Sharad and his computer really got me accustomed more to technology, gave me more exposure, and it's fair to say, I took quite a liking for it!

From Mayank and Ajay, I learned an especially valuable lesson of taking things in my stride and not getting dejected after small losses. In the first few days of our college itself, when the scary monster of ragging was due to come and attack us at any moment, three of us decided to visit a nearby temple to pray for the take-off of our careers. Picture us, three strapping boys in jeans and t-shirts and with large *tikaas* on our forehead, walking back into the campus.

The seniors pounced on us; but Ajay stuck true to his bold and fearless personality and refused to bow down to any of their requests. But, we were marked men (literally marked by our *tikaas*!) and the seniors eventually found us and got us in their grasp; that started a ragging session that went on for 2 months. We were banned from wearing nice clothes, banned from interacting with any girls of our batch or senior batches, and many other such restrictions.

The transition from home to hostel was already difficult for me in those early days, and that felt like the final nail in the coffin for my dying happiness there. But that's when Mayank and Ajay really stepped up to help me. They consoled me that this phase of ragging would pass before I realized it. They helped me realize that it is a part and parcel of college life, and that I should not take it personally; the 3 of us together would tide through it and I would look back and laugh at it. And that's exactly what I do now.

The seniors of my college never intended to really trouble us with their ragging. In their minds, it was like an introduction or initiation ceremony; they just wanted to familiarize themselves with us. Thanks to Mayank and Ajay, those 2 months went by and I stopped being the crybaby that I initially was. And after that, we formed a good relationship with people from all the senior batches.

Even while we were being ragged by one group of seniors, there was always another group that was comforting us-telling us that it was all in fun, and going out of their way to make sure we had enough food in the hostel, faced no trouble in college, or had proper notes to study from.

I still remember that there was a small restaurant where all the seniors would hang around, and it happened to be along the route to the hostel. So I had to cross it every time I exited or entered the hostel, and it used to fill me with anxiety every time.

I felt like a deer trying to escape from the watchful eyes of hungry tigers; I used to be terrified that they would spot me. But they almost always did, and it used to feel embarrassing and upsetting to parrot out the salutations of, *"Good morning, Sir,"* or *"Good evening, Sir"* that they expected from us.

But over time, they welcomed us into the group and I was no longer scared to pass by them. In fact, in the later days, they refused to even let us pay for our own orders. They would playfully clap us on the shoulder and say, *"You are our juniors! You're not going to pay here; we'll take care of it."*

I had never before experienced such pure friendship, and felt like someone (besides my family, of course) was there to look out for me.

One of the fondest memories that remains with me to date is of the long walks that I used to take either by myself, or with my friends. Coming from Delhi, the idea of scenery for me was limited to sky-scraping buildings, luxurious cars, and posh infrastructure.

But in Dehradun, I was exposed to the beauty of nature. Lush greenery, the soft sounds of birds, and clean air were unknown concepts to me. I used to walk up to a telephone booth every day after I first went there to call my mother.

Though I had not yet settled in and started enjoying college and hostel life, those walks became my place of solace. The peace outside calmed me from the inside. When we friends used to venture outside, we had some of the best conversations along those roads. On those scenic paths, surrounded by wonderful people whom I could call my friends, I discovered a new kind of joy and contentment.

Chapter 4

"The great pleasure in life is doing what people say you cannot do"

- Walter Bagehot

My BBA ended in the euphoria of my new-found confidence and positive outlook toward my life and what all I could do with it. A few years earlier, I would have never believed that there would be a right time for me to explore the world out there and try to cement a good place for myself in it.

I was always worried that it would be too soon, I would be too underprepared; I worried that like a caterpillar who breaks out of its cocoon too soon before it was ready, I would crumble and fall, and land up in a worse state than I was before.

But, I now believed that I had some assets at my disposal.I could talk well, engage easily, and compose myself well in public. Additionally, I had gained a steady level of consistency in my education too. I found that with small but regular efforts, studying and getting good marks wasn't half as big of a challenge as the schoolboy in me had made it out to be.

"*Consistency is more important than efficiency*" If you're wondering where this dose of philosophy comes from, it is an original by yours truly. And it is something that I reiterate to myself every day, and something that I believe will help every person fighting to achieve their dreams or ambitions. It matters less if you do 50 things in one day and don't do anything for the rest of the 49 days. What matters more is pushing yourself, fighting all excuses, and getting that one thing done every single day.

It teaches discipline, tenacity, and sincerity in a way that few other experiences can. I had not quite formulated this thought in my head during my student days; but looking back, I firmly believe that it was responsible for the highly satisfactory performance I put up throughout the course.

Thus, imagine me, all hyped up with positivity and self-confidence, with a growing crescendo of upbeat music sounding out the start of great things for me.

But then, a note was played wrong and the crescendo came crashing in a downward spiral.

I was very content with my qualifications and performance, however, recruiters did not seem to agree with my self-analysis. In my mind, I had likened my degree to a golden ticket that would open up avenues for rewarding and well-paying jobs for me.

This was far from the case. I barely had any opportunities, and the good ones were an even rarer find. The job market for new graduates like me was bad, and I found myself sinking in a quicksand of desperation to find a stable job. Since I didn't have the luxury of waiting for too long, I settled for whatever I had in hand; an offer from a call centre.

It was far from the glamourous, fun, or money-minting job that I had dared to dream of. However, I knew I did not have many options at my disposal back then, and so I went into it with all the enthusiasm that I could muster. It was not too fun, but it was something that gave me consistent earnings and the respect that comes with having a stable job. And those things for me were, and remain, very important.

And now, having been through many different kinds of jobs, I have got the perspective that work is work; there's nothing bad or demeaning about any kind of work. It is very rewarding, be it in any form.

I kept it up for a few weeks, and eventually my sister saw through the façade I had created of being content at the job to see how miserable it really made me. She offered to help me find a better opportunity and took me to a job consultancy, where I had hoped to find some desk job.

I still remember that as we were returning in an auto rickshaw, she keenly looked at me and asked why I even wanted to take up a job, when I should instead be pursuing an MBA. That had, in fact, been the first idea I had chased after completing my BBA and I had tried to prepare for the entrance exams. However, I quickly let go of the idea when I realized that my desire to do the course would not materialize into the funds for it; I thought that we could simply not afford it.

My sister's suggestion brought back that dream, and her encouragement helped me overcome my inhibitions. I was worried that an MBA from any college which was not top-level would not be worth anything.

And I had no hopes of getting into a top-level college. She made me understand that the college I graduated from would matter, but not beyond a point. After that, it was just my capabilities that would take me ahead. I took the plunge and attempted the entrance exam with as much studying as I could cram up at the last minute.

I missed the opportunity the first time; my last-minute cramming up simply was not enough. It was hard to accept and easy to give up then, but I decided to take another bet on myself. I prepared again and managed to score 72% in my second attempt, but even that was not enough. I finally decided to enroll for IBS coaching in Chandigarh, and that's how the doors of opportunity for a post-graduate course opened up for me.

I got admission into a school in Chandigarh itself, and took up the opportunity that I had been blessed with through my sister's timely advice. And not to mention, the financial support that she offered, for she paid the first installment of my fees with her hard-earned savings.

Once again, a sibling's guidance proved to be a significant turning point in my life. Indeed, I stepped out of the doors of my campus 2 years later with a highly credible degree attached to my name.

However, there was so much more that I achieved too; intangibles that could not be seen, but which contributed immensely to the person I am today. And truth be told, it was these other aspects that made my MBA experience much more enriching. Instead of simply boosting my resume, they boosted my very personality.

I picked up a lot of leadership capabilities in these final years of my education. The small seed of self-assurance that had been planted in me from my BBA days grew and thrived into a sprawling tree. Instead of slinking into shadows, I felt brave enough to take a step into the forefront.

Instead of approaching people with a dark cloud of an inferiority complex hanging over me, I felt confident that they would like talking with me and would think that I too, am capable of good things. And these changes in my attitude turned my life around completely.

The college too exposed me to a lot of new experiences that helped me flourish. Public speaking and presentation, something that I had devoutly avoided in the past simply because I had assumed I would be no good at it, emerged as my strong suits. It was clear that I had a way with my words; if I used them well, they could take me to the places and get me the things I wanted in life.

With these new skills I had learned in my BBA and MBA, I felt an inherent inner confidence. I walked differently, talked differently, and conducted myself among people differently.

I was no longer the outsider, clinging to walls and trying to hide myself, but instead, I was growing more and more confident to take the centre stage. And this brought a certain amount of popularity my way. People liked me, believed in me, and looked at me in an almost admiring way, like they knew I would do something good in life.

All these factors contributed to my making the decision to run for the student council body of the college. In the world of college, being on that council was like a statement of your influence there, and I wanted to have that kind of influence.

I, along with some dear friends who went out of their way to help me, campaigned enthusiastically. We talked to people, showcased why I would be a good fit for the council, and leveraged the popularity that I had already gained in college. It paid off too, for a large number of people voted for me and I got elected. And once I was on the student council, I realized that I had no idea about what I was doing there.

My motivation to contest the elections was to be popular and be recognized as a member. I had never stopped to think that it was an actual responsibility that I had taken up, and which I had to honor.

I went into it with no knowledge or interest in the important activities that the council did, like budgeting, planning and executing events, etc. The others, realizing this and noticing the lack of initiative from my end in being more involved, gradually started sidelining me (and rightfully so). And unfortunately, I did not have the drive to change that.

In fact, I leveraged my position in whatever ways I could, and tried to do things that I would have never otherwise got an opportunity to do. There was a fashion show being organized by the council, and I insisted that I too wanted to be on the ramp. I did it as a joke, to add an element of humor to the event, but had I not been on the student council, I know my request would not have been entertained. Besides that, I gave a few speeches, but that was the extent of my fulfillment of my duties as a student council member.

My lack of participation in this position which was one of high responsibility gradually started attracting notice, especially from the professors. From every interaction I had with them, I could easily tell that they thought of me as a fluke; as someone who had just happened to win the election but was incapable of handling the demands of the position.

I still remember an incident from those days which has stuck with me. One of my professors, during an event in our college auditorium, said to all the other students from the stage, *"Vikas is a big zero; he can't do anything in life."* I was, thankfully, not present there to hear those words about myself, but I was told of it later.

I could only imagine how his words must have echoed around that huge hall and fallen on the ears of the roughly 250-300 people there.

And the very worst part was, that in the deepest corner of my heart, I couldn't help but wonder that he was right in criticizing me that day. However humiliated and broken I felt, I couldn't shake off the feeling that he had some very valid expectations from me that I did not live up to, and he chose to express his dissatisfaction in that way.

It was painful, but that incident brought with it innumerable lessons for me in coping with difficulties and developing resilience. It also taught me that the casual and carefree attitude with which I had taken up the responsibility of the student council (for it was my lack of participation in that aspect that triggered my professor's dissatisfaction) was wrong; any position of responsibility had to be taken seriously. That has stuck with me for life.

However, I would also like to put forth something here that I hope will benefit other students like me who felt unheard or unseen. Many a times, teachers judge a student too hastily and make up their mind about his or her capabilities based on superficial things. They have been conditioned to equate things like high marks, or being very active in class to success for a student; but that's not always true (speaking from my own example).

Success goes beyond these things too. I wish all my teachers too had taken some time to get to know me, understand my dreams and what I wanted to do, and uncovered the strengths that I possessed; their perception of me and my experiences in schooling and college would have been so different.

However, as they say, time heals all wounds. The wounds inflicted on me by the reality check that my professor's words led me to have healed years later, when I became something in life and received a call from him to be on a podcast.

It was, no doubt, something to be happy about, but my victory was made sweeter by the fact that the call came from someone who had once shown no belief in me. I finally felt seen by him, and we went on to cultivate a very healthy relationship. In a way, he nudged me to never repeat the mistakes I made back then. And whenever I lose sight of the immense power that success wields, in whatever form of it that you may have chosen for yourself, such incidents push me to keep grinding.

On the academic front, I went into MBA believing that I was good in finance. For perhaps the first time ever, I had a dream profession-to become an investment banker. But, life had other plans for me. In my 2nd semester, I jumped at the opportunity of electing investment banking and corporate banking as my subjects. I thought it would be the perfect stepping stone toward my desired career; however, that stone quickly gave way and in a hilarious twist of fate my dreams fell flat on the ground.

Among a large class of 130 students, there was only one who failed investment banking. Me. I always wanted to be one of a kind, and stand out from a crowd; but definitely not in this way!

That was when I realized that finance was not my cup of tea. However, another unexpected avenue opened up for me. It was looking at me all along, waiting for me to catch its eye and realize that that was where my talents lay.

I'm talking about marketing. Quite extraordinarily, I did not choose it as a career but instead, it chose me. While I was chasing behind finance and getting upset at how I performed in it, I never stopped to think for even a second that marketing could be a very good field for me to explore. I was effortlessly getting A grades in it, and I realized later that I have a natural aptitude for it.

The start of my professional career was also in marketing, and it went on to become a significant part of it throughout. I got a job in Evalueserve in the position of an analyst, and my primary role was to conduct market research. Since I had prior experience in calling, I had been selected to conduct telephonic interviews with senior-level executives in various organizations.

A large part of the job entailed me scheduling and getting on long calls that lasted for 30-40 minutes with top executives and asking them a series of questions from a pre-decided questionnaire. Many a times, the calls would get rescheduled or would have to be paused midway if they had other commitments. On paper, it was a marketing job and not a call centre job, but it surely looked and felt like a call centre job.

I never enjoyed calling and did not particularly want to take it up again. However, I still went for the Evalueserve interview, did well in it, and got selected. Though it was not my ideal job, I jumped at the opportunity because it was the opportunity that I got on the very first day of campus placements, and I wanted a job from college.

The environment at the time was rather volatile, and job security was a dream that was not being fulfilled for many. I came to the acceptance that I was lucky to have a job in hand and that I should leap toward the opportunity. I had never before understood that the decision I made was a sign of how maturity had become a part of my personality, and that I had started making thoughtful decisions in pursuit of the big picture. And this approach has helped me out of countless tough spots.

My social life was finally beginning to match the fun scenarios that I had dreamed of after seeing the college bonds portrayed in movies and TV shows. Being on the student council and doing good work there had put me in the limelight, and I was famous in college.

I consider myself very lucky to have found good people who I could call as my friends. Rajendra was a finance genius. Looking back, I think I found it even more difficult to ditch my dream of pursuing finance because I wanted to be like him.

He was extremely talented and the years of friendship with him exposed me to a lot of things. Abhinandan was outspoken and witty, and a wonderful public speaker. He was the type who could sell snow to an eskimo; confidence and charm were the key ingredients that he infused every time he spoke and he truly showed me what impactful speech sounds like.

Both Rajendra and Abhinandan earned a name for themselves in college for their outstanding presentation skills, and they wholeheartedly supported all my experiments and endeavors to up my skill set in this respect. They fine-tuned my speeches, taught me how to put forth my points more strongly, and how to connect better with an audience. Their advice guided me even after college, and to date, I use all the tricks and tips they gave me.

Like many others before and after me, I too caught the love bug during this time. I had been too preoccupied with other, more pressing commitments, to think of romance before this. Between battling my longstanding insecurities, pulling up my socks to do well in my studies, and becoming capable enough to provide for my family, I had never stepped foot into this complicated territory. But changed in my MBA years, when I developed an infatuation with a girl.

I liked her more and more after every interaction that we had, and I naively believed that she reciprocated those feelings. But again, like the countless others before and after me, I was setting myself up for disappointment. However hard I tried and prayed for it, nothing happened between us. I felt very bad, and I must admit, I let petty thoughts take over me and prayed that she too would undergo this same kind of heartbreak.

I would like to believe that I have evolved and matured over the years, for my thoughts on the matter have completely changed now.

Whatever happened, or rather did not happen between us, was equally her loss, and this acceptance made my healing much easier. Instead of feeling rejected by her, I realized that she rejected the chance of good companionship for herself too. And when I started seeing things in this perspective, I no longer held any grudges. Instead of channelling my thoughts toward negativity, I truly wish the best for her now, because my thoughts need to be focused on the many more things I need to achieve in life.

That incident taught me that heartbreak is necessary. For all those of you who have raised a quizzical eyebrow to question my statement, here's the backing behind it. In that phase, when something that I was so hopeful for did not materialize, it gave me a mental shock. I did not know how to trust people or my assessment of their emotions anymore.

I wallowed in despair for a few days. But, (and here comes the part why I say it is good for everyone to experience this), overcoming that mental shock was a big win for me. It taught me that I was more resilient than I gave myself credit for, and that these small setbacks could not derail me. It was a different kind of achievement, but it felt equally special. My emotional strength and maturity had been tested for the first time ever, and I am proud of how I fared in it.

While I got over this incident with time, I never wanted to let the bug come close to me again! I firmly stayed away from romantic endeavors after that. Like in every other major decision of my life, I trusted my family to make the right choice for me and decided I would go for an arranged marriage.

And like always, they came through for me and led me to find the most ideal partner for myself; someone who always has and continues to be the anchor that steadies me against the rough waves of life's many uncertainties and challenges.

Chapter 5

"Shoot for the moon, even if you miss, You'll land among the stars"

- Oscar Wilde

On paper, as I graduated from college with a post-graduate degree in hand, I had everything that a young professional in my place could hope for. I had secured good marks and cleared the final exams, made some very meaningful connections and picked up some invaluable skills from them. Most significantly, I had a job in hand (which not many around me were lucky enough to have). This gratitude for whatever I had been given was alive and pulsing within me and it pushed me to change my perspective about the job I had at Evalueserve.

"Even if it is not your dream job, it's saving you from unemployment, and you can finally start contributing to the family," is what I repeatedly told myself. Like my parents and siblings who had done so much for the family (and especially for me), I too wanted to do something for them. And so, with these consolations, I started the job.

However, I quickly realized that working at Evalueserve was like being stuck in an endless loop. Every day felt the same—sitting at my desk, fine-tuning questionnaires to ask people, making endless phone calls, and then rescheduling those phone calls. In case it is not quite clear from my description, it wasn't exactly thrilling work.

In fact, I kept wondering whether I was looking at it all wrong- I thought it kept money coming into my wallet, but I also wondered whether I was wasting away the money that had been spent on my MBA. I got pangs of panic when I realized that such high sums had been poured into education, and I was now using it to make calls all day long.

One of my colleagues there, who happened to be a batchmate from my graduation days, also wondered out loud to me as to what a highly-educated person like me was doing in that call-centre like job. He meant it in the very best way, but it really got me thinking.

But, I knew I had to stick on with it; this explicit realization, not to mention, the paycheck, made me keep going again and again to the doorstep of the company. I worked to the best of my ability; I was sincere, kept my head down, and continued doing what was required of me. After the initial 6 months there, which were fairly tough to cope with, I eventually got my bearings and I felt an inner peace that somehow, I would make it work there. I also got a small incentive payment; though the sum was not too large, it gave me a certain confidence that I was perhaps doing well there. That intensified my belief that I could make my place there and settle down for the next 2 odd years, after which I would reevaluate my career.

And within a month after this, I was told to not go back there.

The global economic meltdown had struck back then, and claimed me as its unsuspecting victim. Out of the blue, I was called into a meeting room and told I was being laid off. Just like that, my world turned upside down. I had never made false claims to myself or others of loving my job, but I absolutely loved the financial security that it offered me; which I no longer could rely upon.

If I'm being honest, I was quite convinced at the time that it was not only my bad luck that had played a role in getting me laid off; it was also some circumstances created by those around me. As per the company's practices, I was assigned a mentor, whose job was to ensure that my knowledge and skills were honed, and to help me network and shape my career.

The same mentor was assigned to me and another of my batchmates in Evalueserve, and I felt a clear case of unfair partiality unfolding. My batchmate was very conveniently moved out of the Market Research department and into Business Research, which helped him avoid the lay-off.

I naively thought that skill in the job you were hired to do was enough in a workplace; little did I know that I needed to also be skilled in navigating complex workplace relationships and games of politics that went on there.

Ironically, I too had requested to be transferred into Business Research a while earlier through an email that I wrote to my mentor. I take full responsibility that perhaps, my email did not live up to the standards set for professional emailing. I perhaps did not use the right jargon or did not match the crisp tonality needed. However, I feel the outcome was much worse than any mistake I might have made in the email. My mentor severely scolded me in front of my peers (one of whom advised me to actually take action against the unfairness of the mentor), which left me on the verge of tears.

However, it helped me make a very important decision. Whatever else I did or did not do in life, I would give out the same kind of treatment to my juniors as I received from that mentor.

I came to understand that people who do not respect, empathize, and treat others well can never succeed in life (and this was proved by the life arc of my mentor who saw great heights of success in his own venture and then faced a massive downfall).

From then on, I decided that I would never make anyone feel inferior. As an entrepreneur today, I believe that one of my important duties is to get my team working to the best of their abilities, and I seek to do this by offering a positive attitude and the right kind of guidance.

Let me first clarify that eventually, I found my way back on my feet after the lay-off. I bounced back up from the pitfall, and found a way that could get me to the heights that I wanted to reach. I have also now found the maturity to look back at the lay-off as one of the best things to have happened to me.

With the comfort the job offered, it would have perhaps taken me a long time to venture out, explore my capabilities, and try my hand at other jobs. But, the loss of the job forced me to do so, as life's challenges always have their uncanny way of pushing us toward better things. I finally found my way into marketing, wholly and solely, and not remaining within the sidelines of the field as I was at Evalueserve.

Since I've given you the happy ending after this setback that my story found, it is equally important to revisit that difficult time. I knew that a global crisis and some internal politics, both of which I had no control over, had led to me losing my job. And yet, it felt very personal. It felt like my shortcoming, my failure, and my inability to hold a job that I desperately needed. I now wish I had taken more emotionally sound decisions at that time.

I didn't, and even now, I haven't reached the stage where I can call myself emotionally intelligent. My default coping mechanism is not to show any emotions, even when I am at my lowest. I am blessed to have people around me who would gladly offer their love and wisdom; but my first instinct is to hide away from it all. I never let the depth and complexity of my feelings show, and continued fighting by myself to overcome them. So as to not come across as weak to my family, I deprived myself of their support.

However, many good things came in the wake of the lay-off. It nudged me toward a wonderful career where I have thrived over the past 14-15 years, it taught me a lot of things and helped me uncover some traits that I never knew existed within me. After my confidence had fully crumbled, it taught me how to get back on my feet with my head held high.

I started, or rather, I had to start an intensive job search after that. And it was one of the toughest phases of my life. Unknown to me, who was completely a stranger in the cutthroat world that was dominated by internal and unfair politics, the hiring process never seemed to be in favor of applicants. The HR department would keep building pressure, and the managers were notorious for asking very twisted questions that would make you believe you're not good enough.

I wanted to avoid asking my parents or siblings for money at all costs. And so, I eventually took up a job at a start-up that gave me a significantly lesser salary than what I had been earning. However, the founders were kind enough to offer me a chance then. Besides allowing me to handle my own expenses without burdening my family any more, it also helped me rebuild my self-confidence. I worked there for roughly 3 months, after which I got an opportunity in a company in Bangalore.

I worked and lived there for roughly 1 and a half years, and it was quite a difficult time for me. While the work itself was fine (more than fine, for I believe this was the first job that truly kickstarted my career), the city did not suit me at all. The hardcore Delhi-ite in me could just not adjust in Bangalore. The culture, people, and life there was very different from what I was used to.

While the change in setting during Dehradun did me good, this one did not. Most of all, I really struggled with the food, and even my lessons of adjusting to hostel food did not come to my aid. I was falling sick very often, and I was desperately looking for opportunities to move back home. I finally got it, and with it, I got the second opportunity that truly gave my career wings.

Working at Kenscio taught me a lot of things. One of the best things, however, that came from that job was meeting Saurav Patnaik. He was my boss, and the first real mentor who helped me take charge of my career. He invested a lot of time and effort into guiding me, and taught me the ropes of marketing.

One of the most unique experiences that I had with him was that he never treated me like an employee; he always discussed business-related things with me like I was a businessman and that helped me start thinking like a businessman.

He was always very polished and well-dressed, and I saw the effect it had on people around him. I think that is what influenced me a lot to sharpen my appearance and dress well. To date, I use a quality that I saw and picked up from him- while interacting with business leaders, I try to think from their shoes and conduct myself accordingly. He has shaped my career, life, and personality in more ways than I can imagine, and I remain thankful that my paths crossed with his.

The opportunity at Kenscio came to me through luck, chance, and excessive cold emailing. I was desperate to leave Bangalore, and so, I would send out daily emails to every potential source who could give me a job. Saurav eventually reached out to me and asked me to come in for an interview. Things worked out to my benefit, and I was hired as a Key Account Manager for Sprinklr, which has gone on to become a highly successful SaaS company today.

However, back then, the goal was to sell it to enterprises, but not a lot of companies back then had the capacity to invest in as high-tech a platform as Sprinklr was. And perhaps I too was unable to understand the brilliant vision of the CEO. I found the discussions that I had with him very insightful and interesting, but somehow, I could not do justice to the idea he had for the platform.

I was worried that this would reflect poorly on my performance and that I would be forced to lose that job too. It was, once again, Saurav who found me in this state of panic and stress, and saw something in me. He realized that I could do well in some other fields, and brought me on to the account of Headhonchos. My job was to maintain smooth working relations with them and ensure that they got whatever they required from our company.

I dove right into the job and sincerely tried to learn and pay attention to all details. I eventually started making plans and presenting them to top-level executives of Headhonchos. My efforts were received well, and their account eventually experienced a booming growth.

Since I was working so hard to showcase my potential, it ultimately paid off. I was given more accounts to manage, got promoted to a Senior Account Manager, and got a salary hike too.

Business expansion became something that I pondered about day and night; I immersed myself completely into working out something that would expand the accounts that I was managing. I understood that money was a natural by-product of growth. When the business grew, the money automatically grew. This is one learning that I picked up then, and which has stuck with me and influenced my actions even now.

The company and I almost grew together; I was among the few who were with the company right from the start and got to witness its rise. The potential of a dedicated and committed team, like we were, became clearer than ever to me. With a good team in place, no force could stop a business from succeeding; something else that has stuck with me to date.

I was, initially, quite hesitant about a new team member, Sonam Gupta, whom Saurav had hired. I dissuaded him quite strongly before he did it, and was quite convinced that he had made a mistake after he did it. However, I am guilty of having judged and dismissed her too soon (never again have I repeated that mistake). There came a time shortly later when I fell sick for 2-3 weeks, and she really rose to the occasion and handled all my clients so wonderfully. It furthermore changed my mind about what a team can achieve together, with each one looking out for the other, and it was a beautiful feeling to be part of such a team.

I also realized that clients were responding very positively to me because they trusted my intent. When your intention of working for the benefit of clients comes through, it builds an invisible bond between both the parties. Even now, with my investors, it has become a part of my core nature to be very transparent with my intent, and that has worked wonders for me.

Along with clean intentions, it is crucial to believe in what you are saying. I used to think, "*If I am not believing the words coming out of my own mouth, how can I expect anyone else to believe them?*" I also realized how much of a difference it made to my speaking and presentation skills when I was truly convinced about what I was trying to communicate; it was nothing short of a total gamechanger!

While earlier I was chasing the unrealistic dream of knowing everything possible so that people would respond the way I wanted them to, it dawned on me later that all that was needed to achieve that was belief in what I was saying.

The form of leadership that I envisioned after my time there, and which I have inculcated in my own work relies a lot on this. It is still a work in progress, for I have not yet mastered this quality, but I try doing so every day. Leadership is not only about big words and talking; it is about reinforcing the belief in yourself and others that what you are talking and doing is right. Convince yourself that your business is right and that it's going to work; eventually you will manifest it and earn the success that you deserve.

And so, as I mentioned before too, getting laid off was perhaps the biggest blessing in disguise that came my way. It triggered a series of events that helped me meet so many different people, gain so many new experiences, and eventually landed me at Kenscio that gave me invaluable lessons and really improved my people skills, sales skills, and business management skills.

I am incredibly grateful for that opportunity and will always remember that time and those people very fondly.

Chapter 6

"What you choose to do when you have no other option is who you are."

- *Source Unknown*

I'm stating something that is quite obvious by now, but I think destiny had always intended for me to be an entrepreneur. And everything in my life had panned out in a way that helped me fulfil God's plan for me.

Right from my school days, when I felt that I never fit in with the ideal standards of a 'good student' and hence never had any ambitions of being a top-notch doctor or a savvy engineer. As I grew up, my first few steps into taking up jobs did not go as planned.

The mundanity of working in a call centre, the tense and often strenuous environment of Evalueserve (not to mention the rather crushing way in which my journey there ended), and the jobs that I picked up in the startup and in Bangalore right after my lay-off completely satisfied the core requirement that I had from them- they helped me learn and paid me money.

However, it was my job at Kenscio that really made me realize my dream of wanting to be an entrepreneur. Working under Saurav Patnaik was a game-changer in my understanding of businesses. He treated me not just as an employee, but like I was a seasoned businessman. He talked to me about strategies and plans like I had as much at stake as he did.

That's when I came to terms with what I was meant to do—I wanted more than just a job. I wanted to create something, to build something of my own from scratch.

By the end of 2012, I finally decided to take the plunge. After putting aside a lot of inhibitions, and putting together almost every rupee of money that I had managed to save over the years, I started my first venture.

Whenever the doubts started weighing down too heavily on me, I would keep telling myself a learning that I had gotten over the years and which really had helped me whenever I applied it. I told myself that very rare people already possess confidence before they try something new; and that true confidence could only be gained after doing something. With this principle as my guiding light, I set off on this new path.

I decided to start a venture with one of my colleagues. We were working together when we started talking and planning about it on the down low. We eventually decided to invest all our time and attention toward it, and take it out of the cover of secrecy that we had hidden it under. I left my job and within a few weeks, she followed suit.

I can't explain what exactly was going on in my mind, but I had simply assumed that my independence in starting my own venture would not be appreciated by the people who had shown nothing but support and encouragement to me throughout my time there. Even after I had left, we continued operating the business in stealth mode. I wish I had had the courage to be open about what I was doing, and embraced my budding entrepreneurship, especially because I had no reason for keeping it a secret. I perhaps could have benefited from the wisdom of those around me and things might have taken a different turn.

We named our business Manoovar Consulting LLP and we had this idea for a website named 'YourTimeWise.Com' that would send recommendations to users based on their time availability.

We had imagined that we could create a new sensation, wherein our solution would give nudges to our users to visit a nearby mall, spa, or other events depending on how much time they had free at their disposal. It sounded great on paper, but we were quite unprepared practically.

Neither of us had true knowledge or expertise about what we were getting into, and that, I think, proved to be one of our biggest undoing (along with a few other unfortunate factors).

We hired a consulting developer, thinking we would help our business get up and running. But instead, the circumstances were such that he helped to drive it further into the ground. Though he had agreed to work with us, he refused to actually live up to the commitment. He simply started ignoring our frantic calls and messages to him, and never simply never showed up. That was the first blow to our budding business, but there was an important takeaway from it for me. We were heavily relying on this person to use his expertise and support our business, and that is never a wise thing to do. Today, I think twice about doing anything where I am so dependent on someone else's expertise (and I still don't end up doing it!) Because I know that in the world of business, you yourself have to be your biggest asset.

In the meantime, I had left my job and invested all my savings into the venture. I absolutely needed it to succeed.

However, with no established technology, no active users, the limited use of smartphones as compared to today, and two founders who did not have the firmest grasp on what the business required, it turned into a money-draining machine. The graph of my personal savings became lower and lower, but the trajectory of the business remained flat.

Slowly but steadily, after a difficult phase of 6-8 months, we started getting some business and making some money. In my naivety, however, I made a mistake. I decided not to take a salary since I had limited other expenses to take care of, but my co-founder was taking a salary since she was living by herself at the time.

I now understand that such emotionally guided decisions should be kept away from a business. It was a lesson for me to never bring emotions into transactional relationships, and I have stuck with it to date.

When one's family comes under any kind of pressure, it is always the worst to cope with. I got the first exposure to this scary feeling back in 2011 when my mother was detected with a heart problem. I had never imagined her as anything less than a superhero; a pillar of strength, courage, and perfection who could never encounter a problem that she could not solve. But when we heard about this health condition, I realized that my hero needed our support more than ever. It was terrifying but we gradually healed from it, only to be plunged again in the similar situation a few years later.

In the midst of the professional and career-related challenges, my sister-in-law was diagnosed with cancer, and it shook me to my core. I started rethinking about what I was doing in life, and I had made up my mind to distance myself from the business and return to Bangalore. To add to all the things that I was dealing with at the time, I found out that my co-founder had started a similar venture with someone else. She had not been open with me about it; I had caught her at it by chance. Even when I confronted her, she smartly spun a tale of lies and despite knowing that I was being tricked, I just went with it.

The next 2 years of my life were one of the worst phases that I have ever encountered. It was almost like I was stuck in a state of limbo. I wasn't earning any money, I could not find a job, my business was going nowhere, and my business partner was off running her own venture.

Not to mention the catastrophic situation at home that we were all fighting against. I had counselled myself a lot about confidence and how it could be found, but the reality of my life at that time forced me to question those principles I had taught myself. My confidence felt utterly weakened and I felt immensely depressed.

I had hit rock bottom.

Or if there was a place even lower than that, that's where I was. What else would you say about a grown man who needed to borrow money from his mother for a haircut? Or whose mother knew he was absolutely broke and hence used to just quietly give extra money for his basic expenses? The look in her eyes, one that told me she was somehow fully aware of the extent of the mess I was in, made me feel broken.

In the midst of these many financial and emotional difficulties that my brother was dealing with, I unfortunately had to put him through another one. I had to confess that I had lost all my savings and it was one of the hardest things I've ever had to do. I broke down in front of him and cried for almost 2 hours, wallowing in my self-pity. I was young then to understand that feeling bad for myself would not get me anywhere. Till I pitied myself, I would not be able to push myself, and the latter is what truly helped me turn my life around.

Even through everything that was going on, my brother, ever supportive, stepped in. He gave me money to pay off my debts and start over.

For the lack of a more accurate way to describe my feelings, I felt utterly powerless. Not only was I not able to contribute to the family, but I was, once again, burdening them with the additional responsibility of having to bail me out.

I thank the forces that helped me change this situation over the years; I was powerless then but I feel powerful now. I can provide for my family and take care of them the way they did for me. I bought a car for my parents many years later because they did not have a car back then, and that purchase put me on top of the world.

However, till things in my life reached that high, I had quite a few twists, turns, and lows that I yet had to endure.

First things first, my brother advised me to untangle myself from the messy web of Manoovar Consulting. Somewhere deep down, I too had known that I needed to get out of it because I could not even have a conversation with my co-founder without my emotions flaring up. It had gotten very difficult to keep my anger, disappointment, and frustration with her under the wraps.

I took help from one of my cousins, managed to recover some of my money from the venture, and parted ways with her. Despite the outcome, I felt pangs of sorrow sometimes at letting go of the business I had worked hard for. However, I reminded myself of the story of the phoenix; how one has to sometimes completely destroy their old version to build a newer and stronger one. The hope that the same would happen to me too kept me motivated through it all.

I won't try to downplay the negativity I felt toward her back then; it had indeed made a firm place in my heart. But now, I bear no grudges or ill will toward her. I have come to realize that each one of us is fighting our own battles in our own way. I was so caught up in my problems back then that I never stopped to consider her perspective. I was dealing with a lot of my personal problems and she was, perhaps, simply operating from a place of fear when she created a safeguard for herself. Time and experiences gave me this maturity to see things from others' POV too and it has always helped me make better decisions and judgments.

After the help from my brother had somehow got me back on my feet, I once again treaded the path of job hunting. But this time, it felt much more challenging than earlier. Since I was no longer a fresh graduate, simply looking for an opportunity to sustain myself, I was aiming for different types of jobs that came with a certain type of salary and designation.

And that's when I was faced with the very harsh reality that my skill set was quite limited. I knew a lot about how to make money and run a business at a macro level, but I lacked the specific, niche, and advanced skills employers were looking for.

Thus, finding a job proved to be next to impossible. Each rejection hit me harder than the previous one. I eventually understood that I needed to shake myself out of the routine that I had fallen into-

waking up every day and hoping to get a call for an interview or a reply to my emails from any company interested in hiring me.

The thought of setting up another business was daunting, but I realized I had no other option. I couldn't keep waiting for someone to give me a job; I had to create my own path to achieving something in life.

My affinity for marketing had always been strong, and I decided to play to my strengths, unlike the last time when I set up a business in an area that I did not have enough knowledge about. And so, this time, I thought of starting a business in digital marketing, determined to succeed the second time and build something meaningful for myself.

Starting this new venture was incredibly humbling, and it is a journey that will always remain close to my heart. I started out with next to nothing. And I mean that quite literally. I had no office, no setup, no furniture, no companion to work with, and nothing really to work on.

But I did have a lot of motivation that I had to, at any cost, make this venture work. And time showed me that having that motivation compensates for the many other things that you may not have.

I set up a makeshift office. It had just a small *'dari'* which I had borrowed from home which I would sit on, and a broken college laptop on which I tried to set up the workings of my business. Despite the frugal surroundings, I felt a drive and determination to keep at it. I used to meticulously track and calculate my business runway and would write down all the expenses I was incurring everyday. Doing so when the numbers were not in my favor was difficult, but I had enough discipline to keep doing it and hoping that something would change.

I was, and have always been, a believer in the fact that consistent efforts could have a lot of benefits, and that's what eventually turned my luck around. As for the calculations and tracking, it is a practice I have retained to date which keeps me on my toes and keeps me pumped enough to fight.

I eventually started figuring my way around the details of the work I had undertaken, and got a firm grasp of gaining clients. I could present myself confidently, and started coming across as someone who knew what he was doing. One thing led to another, and I got the first real taste of success- a cheque for 17 thousand rupees.

That cheque felt like the first breath of fresh air after being dunked underwater for too long. It was a taste of success, a validation of my hard work, and it gave me a much-needed boost of confidence. With that money, I bought second-hand chairs and a UPS, setting up a more functional workspace.

I hired my first employee and together, we started building the company from the ground up. I hired Biswa as an absolute fresher; he had no knowledge about business and his skills were still very raw. However, he made up for that with his willingness and drive to learn and do better.

There was a point when I had almost thought that I would need to let him go, since I too was struggling with limited budgets, but he really proved himself. He worked hard, and today, he is the CEO of DGTG. I also had two more gems join my team, Snigdha and Sanuj. Their knowledge and integrity in their work was invaluable to me. They really held the fort down and I could, and to date do rely a lot on these three.

It was a slow but steady upward journey. I didn't take a salary for almost two years because I had a weird thought that all of it was mine anyway and I didn't require a salary. I understand now that my thinking was not accurate, and I make decisions in a much smarter and informed way now.

Despite not having any earnings, I kept going and every small step forward felt like a monumental victory.

The experiences, first-hand knowledge in building a business, and other life lessons that these two years taught me largely contributed to what I am today. I still remember an incident that made me feel very powerful and proud of myself, but it was also quite humbling.

I used to do a lot of outreach and networking to gain more business, and in that process, I happened to connect with a lady. I brought out my professional and polite best, and pitched my business to the lady. In return, she scoffed and laughed on the phone and simply hung up. It felt quite hurtful, but I also knew it was a part of the game.

A few years later, that same lady approached me in a way that I would have never imagined- her company had shut down and she applied for a job in my company. It was ironic how the times had changed.

From the many incidents where I was at the receiving end of it and personally experienced how bad it feels, I have always tried to never make anyone feel small or be disrespectful towards others.

Being kind, empathetic, and treating others well might sound like skills not directly relevant to scaling a business, but it helps more than one can ever imagine. I believe it greatly helped me position myself not just as a capable businessman but as a good human being, and that is always appreciated by everyone, be it employees, colleagues, or clients.

And because I understand that nobody is small enough that justifies being rude to them, I also understand that nobody is big enough that justifies being scared of them. I have truly embraced this thinking. You just need to have confidence in yourself, what you are saying, and what you are building your business toward. I have made this a part of my personality, and it has completely changed, for the better, the way I view myself.

In the period from 2014 to 2018, everything that I was earning was poured back into the business. I kept practically nothing for myself, and lived quite a frugal life for those years, but as my business started taking on a better form and size, it all felt worth it. It was the best way

I could spend my funds back then, because the investment I made in my business paid off really well in the future.

My journey of setting up a successful business, full of twists and turns, also taught me what it truly means to be an entrepreneur. Many people can just put in money and set up something; but very few can power through and sustain the hard times to grow whatever they have set up. And that is the true mark of an entrepreneur.

Between that period, I truly learned what being a businessman was all about. I made mistakes and had some wins, and kept trying my best to replicate one while avoiding the other. It took me a couple of years to get it right, but after 2015, I never struggled with the fundamentals of entrepreneurship. I had my share of challenges still, but I never struggled with how to run my business.

I was also fortunate enough to have found some great people who took the business up to new heights, and it's been an onward and upward journey since then.

Chapter 7

"Two little mice fell into a bucket of cream. The first mouse quickly gave up and drowned. The second mouse wouldn't quit. He struggled so hard that eventually he churned that cream into butter and crawled out. Gentlemen, as of this moment, I am that second mouse."

- Catch Me If You Can

I completely meant when I said earlier that after 2015, I never struggled with the basics of how to run my business. I had got a good grasp of what was needed from me as a founder, I had good people with me, and I felt like that front had been covered well.

But, I also meant when I said that I still had my share of challenges. And there were quite a lot of them.

The time between 2015-2016 was quite difficult. I was getting business, but the company was facing a cash crunch almost every 3 to 6 months. It felt like we were barely taking off when the threat of the company going broke would pull us back in. Since it was a fully bootstrapped company back then and we had no funding, sustaining it felt very difficult during these cash crunch periods which would, frustratingly, keep recurring.

I had slipped into the habit of very closely and very often checking the financial situation of the company. I remember that there were at least 2-3 such instances wherein the total money we had left in the company's bank account was lesser than what was needed to give us even a runway of 2 months.

Though it was a struggle we kept going at it. In the meantime, I had taken it upon myself to explore and find new people who could contribute to the company and new sources of revenue that we could tap into.

I had some idea about the fields of email and social media marketing, but mobile & video advertising, media buying on Facebook & Google, etc. were alien concepts to me. But I knew they would be important for my business and hence, I hired people for it. Gradually, DGTG could expand into these new streams too, and the challenges and opportunities that my business had kept balancing each other to give it a rather steady state.

Somewhere in 2017, my business sustained a heavy blow, almost to the tune of 35-40 thousand dollars. And what made it worse was that the blow felt somewhat personal too because it came from someone whom I considered a friend and used to look up to.

He was one of our clients, wherein we were selling traffic to him on the basis of clicks and he was buying for conversions. His entire business model entailed selling products for very low prices and monetizing it by getting traffic from companies like ours.

Since we were still reasonably new in the business, we were giving him credits worth almost 15-17 lakhs month on month. It was big business, but our margins for it were very thin, barely 10-15%. At the start, the money would get paid to us after a cycle of 30 days, but it just kept getting pushed and pushed till the cycle became of almost 90 days.

At one time, the total billings amounted to almost 25-30 lakh rupees. I too had taken credit from some people, and the client (also my friend) kept lying to me and delaying the payment. Eventually, he just vanished and since he was personally known to me, he told me how his business had collapsed and how he had no money left to pay me.

In my naivety and trust in him, I took his word and just let it go. However, that turned out to be a big mistake, because I soon came to know that he had started another business and settled almost $1/10^{th}$ of the debt that I had to pay from my own pocket. And so, my mistake of blindly trusting in people set me back by several thousand dollars.

However, even through those difficult times, I did not disappoint any of the suppliers. I went and met each of them face to face, explained the situation and tried to get them discounts. I eventually paid all their costs too, which I had expected my client to do.

I sometimes wonder whether he was genuinely stuck in a problem that he could not find his way out of, but what I was seeing in front of me made that quite confusing to accept. Whatever may have been the truth, it surely left me with a lot of important lessons and gave me the inherent confidence that I could handle things even when they were out of control.

This setback almost wiped out my business. I had learned that typically, many new startups went out of business because of a few causes. I had already experienced the downfall of Manoovar Consulting due to a partner fallout. I knew that the second thing that could push a bootstrapped and non-funded company like mine out of existence was low cash availability. And I was determined to not let this happen.

I was able to pay off that massive and unexpected expense from some reserves that we had saved up over time. But that took away funds worth almost 7-8 months of runway for the company. If someone would have told me a few years before this that my company would face a Death Valley situation (the term used for when a startup is on the verge of losing all its reserves), I don't know how I would have reacted, for even thinking about those used to haunt me.

In that entire phase, I was very worried about my startup dying and used to keep wondering how I could sustain it, but I found a kind of strength within myself.

I truly believe that if your intent is right, you're doing the right things, and you're being honest with your work and the stakeholders involved in it like your partners, employees, clients, and suppliers, it will always come to your aid. I cannot really explain how it works, but I can personally vouch that it happens.

We bounced back from the hit that the business took and managed to sustain a good trajectory over the next 2-3 years. We squeezed out profits and maintained a low burn rate. I would see a lot of my competitors and contemporaries going out to international locations to take part in business meets and conduct events.

I really wanted to do that too, but I kept my head down and prioritized earning large sums of profits. I had a very clear vision about how much I wanted to save up in the business and how large of a reserve I wanted to create. It should be enough to keep the company alive for 3-4 years even if we stopped actively doing business.

I worked hard toward this and I feel very lucky to have had a great set of people working alongside me. Nothing would have been possible had it not been for the wonderful team I had put together at DGTG, and together, we built something that we were all proud of. Eventually, there came a time when the aftereffects of our Death Valley situation were completely gone. We were sustainable and had finally succeeded in creating a reserve that would help the company survive for a couple of years without business.

It was at that time, roughly three years after I started my solo entrepreneurship journey, that I felt stable in my career. I knew that whatever else came my way, I was at a point where I could take care of myself and my family. And that's when I made the decision to expand my family.

It was, strictly speaking, not my decision but more like my agreeing to my parents' decision. They had been pushing me toward getting married for a while before that. But since I did not have anyone suitable in my life, I would avoid it and kept giving excuses like, *"I'm not making enough money on my own,"* or that *"I cannot take on an additional responsibility."* But eventually (and by God's grace) there came a time when these excuses did not stand true and I decided to give in.

Having seen some really difficult and stressful times in the years before 2018, I was not at the pinnacle of fitness. I was overweight by almost 10-15 kilograms and I knew I was not looking my best. I still had phases when I did not feel the best either, when the pressure of running a business and the constant back-and-forth cycles that are typical for startups used to get to me.

But despite that, I felt confident about me being a good option for anyone in the marriage market to consider. I was earning my own money, I had my own car, and my own house. In fact, I had everything that I wanted to have at that age. And I thought that would help people see me as a very suitable companion. However, a lot of people did not seem to think like I did.

Like for any bachelor in those days, the process started with creating profiles on sites like Shaadi.com and Bharat Matrimony. I saw very specific requirements placed by the parents of the women whom I was interested in, and a lot of them entailed having a secure job.

Though I was earning well, being an entrepreneur somehow did not evoke confidence in many of the people I met. Today, thanks to the growing popularity and even the support being given to startups, they've got a certain level of credibility and glamor linked to them. But this was not the case a few years ago.

There was a woman who I met and talked to for almost 2 weeks. My family and her had already met and liked one another and so I kept thinking that it would materialize into something. During one of our meetings, I poured my heart out to her and very honestly told her that along with being an entrepreneur, I also invested in other ventures and that a lot of my money at the time was in high-risk startups.

My honesty turned out to be my undoing. She ghosted me completely after that. When I asked her sister about it, I realized that the girl had thought of me as financially unstable when I opened up to her about my work and investments.

But I don't think of this less as rejection, and more as natural selection. People who were not the right match for me got filtered out, and I eventually met my life partner, Shweta. She is someone who has stood by me for many years and supported me through everything.

I was in a comfortable, but not too lavish, financial state when I met her and she chose to put her faith in me. With her by my side, I grew and prospered a lot, and have been able to give her a good life.

Before I met Shweta, all the prospects that had not worked out for me had made me feel quite upset. Many of my friends too were married by then, and I had put an unnecessary kind of pressure on myself. As they say, the best things in life for you have a way of eventually finding you. Funnily enough, Shweta was working at Shaadi.com at the time and fate (as well as our families) eventually led to us meeting.

She was one of the only women who I had met who respected the entrepreneur in me. She never probed me about how much I was earning, how stable my business was, or what exactly I did. In fact, even to date, she is happy not knowing the nitty gritty of my work!

All of my previous encounters with women had made me feel like I genuinely did not have anything (which was far from the truth). She sparked that belief in me again that I was standing on my own two feet, I was capable, and I had achieved things in life. And what better qualities could I have asked for in a wife?

What really drew me to her was that she never had any problem with the high-risk nature of my work. She was, at the time, a very independent woman and financially secure since she was in a job. But despite that, she never made me feel like I was not equally stable through my business.

I think it really helped that her father too ran his own venture (that of a local newspaper) and she had seen in her home what it took to run a business. Or perhaps, it was her own inherent maturity and goodness that she wholeheartedly supported my work.

The only thing that really mattered to her was that I too shared her love for travelling. We travel together to many places now, gaining new experiences and making our bond better and stronger!

Call it lady luck or the culmination of many years of hard work, but my business really took off in the couple of years that followed my marriage. Our revenue grew by 2-3 times.

I always had a tendency (and I think many of you must have felt it too) that seeing success of any kind for others makes us feel like we are getting late to achieve it. Be it someone who got married, or someone who got a great investor on board, or someone who bagged a very big client. My constant thought was, *"When am I going to get all this? Why is it not coming to me?"*

Somewhere along the years, and I think it was mostly in that very challenging and transformative phase between 2015 to 2018, I got the wisdom that things will happen when they are meant to happen. There's nothing we can do to speed it up, all we can do is patiently and diligently keep working toward whatever we want.

Around this same time, I had also started investing and supporting other startups. One of the founders whom I invested in was a young and dynamic guy named Prabhdeep Singh, who is still a very dear friend.

He got me interested in the world of E-commerce and his idea of drop shipping. I am so glad I could be the person for him who I wished someone had been for me- I told him I believed in him, that I would invest in his idea, and asked him to move to Bangalore. He came, along with his friend Utsav (who went on to become my co-founder), and we started working together in Bangalore.

I was finally doing something that I enjoyed. My business was succeeding. I was on my way to making the money that I had always dreamed of and using it to create a good life for me and my family. I had a solid team in place whom I could rely upon and grow with. And that's when the Covid struck.

I had invested a lot in a new office just days before the lockdown was announced. Not only was it heartbreaking to know that the office could not be used, but it was also quite difficult at first. Large companies often have dedicated people to handle different areas, but for a startup, everything rests on the founder. It was on me to handle emergencies like that one and get myself and my team used to the work from home system.

For the E-commerce business, we had acquired a lot of stock from China that was to be sent to the USA, but all those services also got stopped. I had put in almost 8-9 lakhs in it, and this plus the investment made in the office that lay abandoned was a double whammy that hit me.

To make matters worse, DGTG also started losing money because we simply could not get clients in that time. I still remember that one dreaded month when our revenue dipped by almost 95-98%. I knew I desperately had to do something, but I did not know what.

I started with the very basics and began reaching out to every person on my team. I would offer my support and my help, though in reality, I had still not figured out how I could help them if it really came to that. But I just wanted to let them know that I had their back.

I knew how worried I was about the situation and realized that the worry must be much more for them because they perhaps felt like they would lose their jobs.

One of my proudest accomplishments is that throughout the many months of the lockdown, DGTG retained each and every of its employees. Salaries were paid on time (though we had to make minor deductions), even bonuses for festivals were given, and I could give that financial security to everyone who worked with me.

In fact, there were some employees who we had planned to remove due to their non-performance, but even they were retained during that phase. From home, I even procured medical insurance for the team.

Honestly, I did not know whether this was expected or required of me. But my natural instincts just told me to do whatever I could to help out others. My thinking was that if I took these measures today,

I could avoid problems for the future in case someone would have really needed any treatment. I wanted to ensure that nobody felt helpless and desperate for their health.

While I was trying my best to take care of my business family, my own family faced many difficult times. Somewhere in May 2020, Shweta's father got detected with cancer. It was emotionally, mentally, and physically very draining, especially since our hands were largely tied because of the ongoing pandemic. We did whatever we could; I made calls to whomever I knew who could help us in that situation. Unfortunately, I too came down with a severe skin infection at that time that lasted for 2-3 months.

I felt very scared and used to get very negative thoughts at that time. And what made it more difficult was that I could share them with anyone. Shweta was grappling with her own stress and tension over her father's health. My parents were living by themselves in Delhi in the middle of the pandemic with no support or help available, and hence, I could not burden them with my own problems.

I know this time was very challenging for many others too, like me. Between 2020-2021, every possible problem that could come my way, be it health and mental health problems, financial problems, and leadership problems wherein everyone just expected me to have answers but I had no one whom I could ask my questions to. I had no choice but to figure out things for myself.

In 2021 we lost her father. It felt like I had been put back into a horrible pit of memories because it was like another horrible time that my family had already gone through. My sister-in-law too had succumbed to the same disease, and I was not prepared to cope with the loss of another family member to cancer.

If you ask me today how I did it, my honest answer would be that I don't know. I don't know if I have the strength to deal with such traumatic times. But looking back, I also realize that we often remain unaware of our full capacity to take on and handle things. We don't know the limits to our will power; it gets tested and, in a way, unleashed to its full potential only when things get tough.

I have always been blessed to have the support of my family in every phase of my life. Be it my parents who gave their all to give me a good life, or my siblings who put me on the right career path, or my wife who has stood by me like a rock.

Why that phase felt even more challenging was because I felt like I could not ask them for that support. It was up to me to be there for them, and even all the people of my company, and that thought of having so many others relying on me used to worry me, mostly because I did not want to fail anyone.

If you remember how I talked about life and time being the most impactful and effective teachers, the 2 years of Covid really drove this point home. I felt like I matured by many many years in that duration and became a stronger version of myself.

Chapter 8

"The people who are crazy enough to think they can change the world are the ones who do."

- *Steve Jobs*

The years of my life from 2015 to 2020 felt like a rollercoaster that I had been made to sit on. I am, and will always remain grateful for many of the things that happened to me during that time. However, those highs came with a lot of difficult and devastating lows too. My family, my business, and I were put through some major challenges. But I am happy that all of us made it off that crazy ride with a lot more strength and resilience.

In terms of my business and the role of an entrepreneur that I had chosen for myself, a few things became crystal clear to me during that time. Saving a business from a massive cash crunch and making it survive through a global pandemic comes with a lot of learning lessons. I would like to share those with all the entrepreneurs who happen to come across my story so that whatever may come in the way of you and your business, you can find yourself more prepared to deal with it.

One of the most significant lessons I got was about the importance of profitability. We have always been told by our parents that a good education is like a security blanket that will always remain with you and help you when needed.

For a business, having a good accumulation of profits is the security blanket. Be it in unprecedented circumstances like Covid, or situations that a company may commonly face such as a slowdown of business, a reserve of profits will always come to your aid.

I put this theoretical lesson into practical implementation, and we managed to build a runway for the business for more than two years. This happened because I became very frugal; spending money only when and how much was absolutely necessary and putting back everything else into creating more business and more profits that would ensure we never had to worry about our survival if the hard times came back.

Secondly, I realized that there was no real 'stopping point' when you're an entrepreneur. There never can (and never should be) a time when you feel that you've explored everything regarding your business. You need to be on the constant lookout for new sources of revenue and always be thinking about what you can do next.

As an entrepreneur, you need to be constantly evolving for only then will your business evolve and expand. It was one of the biggest achievements of DGTG that we managed to do so beautifully within those difficult 5-6 years.

And the last part was about bracing yourself and preparing to take quick and maybe even drastic measures for the good of the company. How you build a team and what kind of people you have on the team makes all the difference. It is the foundation upon which your business's success can stand.

Somewhere between 2019-2020, I began seeing that a few people had become redundant to the operations and efficiency of the company. We needed fresh talent, and so, we kept hiring and experimenting with new people. This is a process that never ends, and to date, I am constantly in search of people who can bring something new to the table and do better than even I can. I know that's the best way for my business to grow.

The first few months of 2020, till the lockdown struck, was the most transitional period of my life. I had met Prabhdeep and became very interested in the idea of an E-commerce store that he had come to me with. I had accumulated some wealth, I was investing in a lot of new people, ideas, and businesses, and I felt like I was in a comfortable space to do so while ensuring I could make it through whatever other challenges may come my way.

And as you know, quite a lot of challenges came my way. My investment of approximately 20-30 lakhs in the new office space was just wasting away because the Covid lockdown had been announced just two days after we had inaugurated the office.

I had also put in quite a lot of money in the drop shipping, but that too had come to a standstill. The lockdown was responsible for this too and it was a problem that I simply could not find my way out of, because it was much, much bigger than me or my business.

But, there was some good waiting to happen even then. Such experiences have really made me believe in the idea that every dark cloud does have a silver lining.

During that period, Prabhdeep introduced me to one of his friends, Utsav, who went on to become my co-founder in the venture that I run today.

Utsav was a very naïve and simple person. Like me, he was also excited at the idea of the E-commerce store. Just before the lockdown was announced, Prabhdeep had left Bangalore and returned to his hometown of Delhi. But Utsav was stuck in Bangalore for those 2-3 months, and that's when he introduced me to PUBG.

The popularity of PUBG was spreading like wildfire back then. It was picking up a lot of momentum in India and that sparked a wonderful idea for Utsav. I was very intrigued and impressed by it, but little did I know how it would change the direction of my life!

He told me that he had thought of organizing tournaments through an application. The app was not required to be too complex to develop, maintain, or operate. It needed an investment of just 10-15 thousand rupees and I happily gave it to him because I was curious to see how the idea would pan out and wanted to take a chance of exploring this new field.

Utsav promoted the tournament and app using influences, social media, and whatever other methods were feasible in those days. But it worked wonderfully and we got downloads of over 1,70,000 within the first 2-3 months itself! That was the starting point of ESportsXO, which went on to become one of India's fastest growing E-sports organizations.

But in the initial phase, we had not quite realized what we had started and how big it could become. For those first 2-3 months, we were just toying around with the idea and not really looking to scale it. But I was hooked onto the idea and I gradually started thinking about it more and more.

Back in 2019, I had visited South Korea and got a chance to attend a very famous event named G-Star. It is focused on the gaming industry and is like an annual trade show. Since then, I had been intrigued at the idea of starting a product company.

My work till then had always been service-related and so, the idea of diversifying into something product-related excited me. And the thought of doing something like that in gaming made it even more exciting for me.

You may perhaps be wondering what it was about gaming that drew me to it.

I wanted to create something that would impact a lot of people. For a long time, the only thing that came to everyone's mind while talking about 'keeping people connected' was social media. But, I knew that while social media platforms did really create a good network of people, each one had its life cycle. Orkut gave way to Facebook, and then Instagram. I did not want to simply make another temporary thing, a fad that would die down with time and be replaced by something else.

I strongly felt that gaming environments offered something different. They were like a Metaverse where you could pick your name, be whoever you wanted to be, and look however you wanted.

Having personally felt what it was like to be picked on (speaking from my school days) for simply being yourself and not aligning with what others expected you to be, I felt this was a very freeing and empowering world. Nobody was confining anyone to act in any way, or be someone that they were not. The idea of creating such a world for others excited me.

Players could hang out, exchange ideas, and even meet offline. It was socializing made easy. It connected people who would perhaps otherwise not find any common ground and created a community within itself. Even as I continued playing from my phone in my home, I felt I had made new connections and found a new tribe for myself.

I envisioned that gaming would become the next big thing like social media. When I found out that 2.6 billion people were actively using it, I believed that creating value for gamers was the key to success. By providing them with a platform to play, and allowing developers and creators to connect with gamers, I could create value for both the involved stakeholders.

Driven by this desire, I decided to take a leap of faith to see if and how we could grow this small-scale but popular venture that we had started. Feeling good about it and about what we had set out to do, we registered the company in June 2020. And in August 2020, PUBG was banned in India. This was a big setback, and unfortunately, another one over which I really had no control.

Overcoming the severe and simultaneous problems that came to my business and my family, not to mention my own health problems had changed something in me without me having even realized it. I had just become wired to keep going through anything and everything.

When you're in the middle of a problem that you cannot solve, but you also don't want to give up, the only remaining option is to go with the flow and take one day at a time. That's what I did. I gradually got a hang of how to run a gaming business.

In the few months between June to August of 2020, there was another person involved in the company and its work, whom I had not even met yet. That was Rohit, my other co-founder. Though he was a co-founder, I did not end up meeting him till 2021, when he eventually came to Bangalore. Rohit had come with a strong understanding of technology and he too was very taken up with the idea of creating a product in the gaming industry.

He initially started working on something called 'Battle XO' but we were failing in it because we did not have the right kind of people to actually build it. Rohit had a good grasp of technology and understood the logic, but he was not a coder. He took this up later and actually learned coding and product management and today, he is the CTO and CPO of the company.

Both him and Utsav eventually relocated to Bangalore and as we started full-fledgedly working toward this, it felt like I had finally got the moment that I had been waiting for all my life. But by this, I don't mean to say that the journey was completely smooth sailing and easy!

We were spending quite a lot of money without even realizing it. I had invested almost 120-130 thousand dollars into it by then but we were still not seeing the kind of traction that we wanted to see.

Around September-October of 2020, when the game had been banned, two more members of our current team had also come on board. Naman and Nayan both came with a lot of expertise and understanding of how the gaming ecosystem works.

We envisioned an idea of a gaming house and we wanted to make it the biggest in India. It was a huge villa of 10,000 square feet named "XOSpace", and it was in the middle of the city. It was a space where 10-15 content creators would play, stay, and it was like a hostel environment.

This gave us a lot of traction, media attention, and even a closer understanding of how the gaming industry works. We were being noticed by investors too. Having just got a glimpse of how big it could turn into and what we could actually achieve, my desire and drive to grow the business further also grew.

And again, I was out back onto the rollercoaster. I was going higher and higher, doing something that I felt good about with good people. But I had another period of lows waiting for me, that was once again triggered by the pandemic.

April to June of 2021 was again a rather tough period. Money was not coming in easily, we had a lot of costs, especially those of XOSpace which was also taking up a lot of my personal resources as well. At that time, I began hearing a voice in my head and heart that was telling me to give up.

But the voices around me, of the wonderful team that we had put together, helped me overcome that feeling and we made a choice to secure the future of our business. I could not keep funding the costs of the business endlessly, especially if we wanted to make it big. And that's when we decided to raise money.

We needed someone who could back our business for the long term, understand the ecosystem, and actually help us make a place for ourselves in it.

Running a business in gaming for almost a year and a half without being funded was a real struggle. What I believe really helped me through it all was constantly learning and improvising. Every entrepreneur brings a certain number and type of skills to the table. But as I said earlier, entrepreneurs can never stop! You need to keep building on those skills and evolving, and that's exactly what I did too.

Soon after we had decided to raise funds, we had the first call toward it sometime around the month of June itself. It was a startup accelerator that was giving us money through SAFE notes. Now, to start with, we did not even know what SAFE notes were. We were rejected on that first call itself which was very disheartening. Having had zero experience with the process, I could not pitch our business too well. I went with a very basic pitch deck too.

While I was familiarizing myself with this new process, I would take almost 3-4 days of prep and practice for a 20-minute pitch. I would end up speaking very fast, with my words crashing into one another, and I did not feel confident enough. But I kept going. I did around 15-20 pitches and though I kept getting rejected, I felt my confidence grow with time.

We also got a lot of mentors who came at that time and advised us about how to build and grow our product. We met Rakesh, our current Advisor for Technology, during that phase and he helped us a lot to build momentum on the tech side and guided us on how an enterprise product should be built.

I also gained a lot of valuable advice and lessons from some good investors. Though they rejected me, they left me with many important learnings.

All in all, those few months were very intense. We needed to continuously improve ourselves, showcase ourselves in the best light, and not get disappointed when things didn't go our way. However, we finally caught a break after 6 months; in December 2021, we got our first cheque.

For this, we had to go through almost 140 pitches and we made 16-17 different versions of the pitch deck. I still remember that delighted and exhilarated feeling I had when I finally got the call saying 'Yes!' to us from WeFounderCircle. I will always remain grateful for the help and support we received from them. They also opened more doors of opportunity for us and introduced us to another investor called SOSV (today, known as Orbit Startups).

From the way the pitches went, it seemed like both these investors made a decision quite early on to put their faith in us, and that's exactly the kind of momentum we were looking for. We were looking to raise 300,000 dollars but we got oversubscribed by almost 3x and ended up raising around 1.1 million dollars in our first round of funding!

At that time, I felt so happy that I believed I was at the peak of my career. I felt that each and every of those 140 pitches that we had to go through was worth it, because it helped us get something bigger than what we had even hoped for back then. It truly felt like our business had been given a new (and very solid) lifeline because it came to us just in time, when our previous reserves were almost running dry.

And from there, another journey began that I had never experienced before- the journey of running a funded startup. Along the way, I picked up many new and useful skills of presenting myself well, sounding more confident and reliable, and I believe these soft skills are an important asset for any entrepreneur.

I had been very excited yet nervous about the idea of raising money, and here's why. I had always considered myself an underdog. I was not a naturally brilliant student, gaining education from Ivy League schools and colleges.

The idea that someone (other than my family, of course, who did this for me multiple times) would take a bet on me and actually invest in ME felt like it would be the ultimate seal of approval for myself about how far I have come.

When we raised that money, it finally felt like I had won in life! We were celebrated and people talked about us like we were the next big thing to look out for, and it was the best feeling ever.

I finally was seen by my friends and acquaintances in the light that I always wanted to be seen in. I had proved that I really did have something in me. And that my journey was far from over! I had many more challenges like harsh investment winters to overcome, but I had many more wins to claim too!

Chapter 9

"The difference between a fighter and a warrior is that warriors fight for two extra minutes."

- *Source Unknown*

It's pretty easy to understand that when you're stressed, under pressure, or things aren't going the way you want, you end up making mistakes. I had never really experienced the other side of things, where everything was going exactly as planned, and my life felt like a complete and beautiful puzzle—until after our first big fundraise. That was the first time I realized that even when everything seems perfect, you can still make mistakes.

And I made some mistakes too.

I was on a high from my success, something I had always dreamed of. But this made me feel like I had reached a level where no problems could affect me. It was the first real win of my life. And it was a win worth millions! The feeling was something I had never experienced before, and naturally, the situation caught me by surprise.

I have admired Shah Rukh Khan for the longest time, and it is for much more than his exceptional acting. I admire the way he built himself up, how he overcame all odds, and the man that it has made him. During one of his speeches, I heard him say that after getting the first glimpse or a small amount of success, that's when you need to start working even harder and remain patient.

I did not really understand the depth behind this statement when I first heard it. If I had, I would have been on my guard to not make those same mistakes.

For a brief period after that December in 2021, I started thinking that I had reached the ultimate zenith of what I could achieve. I think without me even realizing it, I became that small school boy who hesitated to ask his parents for a pair of shoes, or that college student who could not live up to the first test of responsibility as a student council member. All those versions of myself that I had once been crept up in me.

I started looking at that victory like that small school boy or that young college student. The entrepreneur in me had grown and evolved from these versions. And so, seeing that cheque in my hands, I just let myself give it to the elation that I was feeling. I kept thinking back about all those years, and comparing just how far I was at that time as compared to where I had started out my journey from.

And while I was doing that, it actually hit me that I had come very far.

I had struggled a lot, fought against myself and others to overcome challenges, and I finally started feeling like I had done enough. I felt like I could give myself the chance to just rest for some time and catch my breath.

But here's what I think ended up happening: I had been in a race against myself and against time for so long that when I let myself take that small bit of rest, I found it difficult to get up and running immediately again. I kept hitting snooze on the alarm clock, just wanting to enjoy that win for a little while more.

And that's when I wish I had understood that I had chosen a rather improper time to take my rest. As my idol actor, and perhaps many others before him had realized, having tasted success only meant that you needed to start grinding more.

For a business, the responsibility increases by almost 10 to 20 times after you raise money! It's because you are now not only responsible for your vision and your team, but also for the people who have believed in your vision.

Now, I don't mean that you should not savor the victory of a fundraise! Having personally seen the immense effort, sleepless nights, and practice that it takes to make a pitch perfect, securing an investment is definitely worthy of being savoured. But this needs to be a momentary celebration, from which you quickly go back to working hard.

My party lasted just a little bit longer.

When we raised the money, the platform that we wanted to build had not existed. It started coming into shape only somewhere in February 2022. We were hiring tech people as well as other support staff. We did it all in the rush to start growing the company. But we had not properly mapped them to the roles that they would play in the future of our company.

And that's when the words of another founder friend of mine became so applicable to me (though I had not realized it at the time). He had told me to become extremely frugal after raising money. When I had first heard this, I had thought to myself, *"Maybe that's just his story and his experience, and it is not related to me."* But this is applicable for every entrepreneur and every business!

A very easy mentality to slip into while hiring is to think that, *"I can get in so much business, and then these people will be useful assets."* But this mentality is also dangerous! Because it can make you just keep hiring more and more people in the belief that you may need them at some point in the future. And that's not the best way to spend away your funds.

We also invested quite a bit in fixed and immovable assets. While taking a new and bigger office, we justified it to ourselves with the reasoning that it was okay for us to have a larger space because we had a bigger team, and we were working on creating a new studio in Delhi. This took up almost 4-5 months of our time, not to mention a lot of funds too.

I started realizing that almost 10-15% of our money had been tied up in immovable assets and that's when I started pushing and gearing up the team to start building up now.

But back in Delhi, a lot of people were still being hired. The founders were in Bangalore and we were not physically there to oversee the day to day operations. How much ever connectivity and interactions can be maintained online now, it does not compare with the actual presence of a founder at the ground level.

This experience made me understand that a founder must always take the onus of controlling the company. By this, I don't mean that a founder should micromanage, but needs to be there to look at what is happening on the ground.

During all this, there was still a lot of work from home being done, which further reduced the face time of the team with us founders. 2020 and 2021 had been extremely brutal years. An atmosphere of fear had taken over, and the reports from the media about a new surge being expected or the lockdown being put in place again did not help. I too was scared and I was not prepared to take the risk upon myself of having the team in the office.

We had also put in a lot of money into the gaming house, and that expense was becoming hard to sustain. Ultimately, in December 2022, we shut it down. This decision came with the realization that it was a cost center which we had built but it was not making us money.

I had, in my early days as an entrepreneur, formed a thesis in my mind that you have to always start with some revenue and profits in mind. There has to be a goal to eventually make profits at scale of whatever you venture into. But, I think this thesis of mine got sidelined somewhere along the way and I ended up reconnecting with it rather late. I got sidelined in the race and buried under the pressure of achieving immense growth and raising the next round of funding.

While we were caught up in these things and looking focussing on the big picture of actually expanding the company, the market was not waiting for us. It followed its own dynamic course and from the period of December 2021 to June 2022, it changed tremendously.

We began hearing talks of the 'Great Investment Winter'. In the literal sense of its name, investments simply get frozen in such a time.

I happened to come across a very interesting article posted by Y Combinator about this and in a nutshell, this is what it told me: Raising money is going to become difficult. And the startups who are here, in the grind, should know that they did not build the startup of fundraising. They should remember the reason why you started it in the first place.

Nobody was really willing to put in money into startup ventures, and that's when we started seeing a downward trajectory. We started regretting why we had made so many big expenses earlier, but unfortunately, our strong regret could not get the money back. There was nothing else we could really do except for waiting till it blew over.

Back then, we were in the Accelerator Programme of Orbit Startups. We were gearing up for a pitch in front of them somewhere between May-June and by then, news of the funding winter had already started spreading. Fundraising, which was an already difficult process, was made much more difficult by the fact that investors now had a much more cautious and guarded mentality because they knew how the market was shifting. The market was to become very tough for startups that were not healthy or in a bad shape.

I have come to realize one very important thing, which I have also heard from many investors. If it's a healthy startup that is given money, it will grow and become healthier. But, if the startup is basically damaged, with a mismanaged or no proper business model, or a startup that is not managing cash flow and finances properly, it will suffer and perhaps become damaged if it is given money.

So the math is very simple: If the startup is in a good condition, the funds can make it better. If it's in a poor condition, the funds can make it worse.

And this is a rule that opened my eyes, and something that I still use to guide my decisions and actions. Regardless of whether we get or do not get funds, my priority is to make it a good and healthy company.

It went on for almost 2-3 months. By the time August came, we were gearing up to get out of our slump and preparing for a fund raise again. But, other plans were in store for us.

The government banned the game BGMI and this was a very big blow for us. We had invested almost 50-60% of our funds and we had very little cash in hand. We had a very big project in hand, worth almost 2-2.5 crores, and we heard the news of the ban just 2 days before we were to kickstart it.

The problems kept coming but the solutions did not. We had a team of almost 70 people relying on us. Our burn rate was very high. And we just did not know what we could do.

Remember the feeling I described that my life felt complete like a beautiful puzzle? Piece by piece was suddenly being taken apart and I was breaking internally.

We desperately needed to find a way to turn the company around.

What's worse was that we were getting good offers, and that kept giving us false hope. Because none of them were actually getting converted in terms of financing and funding.

During a Demo Day presentation, where I had to pitch to almost 150 investors online, our company was the only one that got more than 35 interests. Among the 15-16 startups that I was competing with, we had garnered the maximum interest. I was ecstatic, and I thought that this would be the lifeline we needed.

But I soon started seeing that while we were prepared enough to draw that interest, we were not prepared enough to actually convert it. We were seeing the looming threat of another Death Valley in front of us and circumstances just kept pushing us closer and closer toward it.

We were struggling to survive with a runway of barely 1.5 months. I increased my efforts a lot to raise money. Think of someone who does not know how to swim and who has been pushed into the waters. Without knowing whether it will work or not, the person will just keep beating and moving their hands and legs, just struggling to stay afloat. That's pretty much how we were.

We did not know what would work but we had to keep trying something. We kept pitching. I loaned some of my personal funds to try to bail out the company. But the damage had run quite deep. We had sustained a loss of almost 1.5-2 crores.

I had already dealt with many challenging phases in my journey as an entrepreneur. But something about this one felt different.

The banning of the game, which led to our big project getting impacted, which led to the depletion of company funds, which made us desperate to find sources of funding, which was made impossible by the funding winter. And to top it all, we were realizing the mistakes we had made in the way we spent our earlier funds. I had never had so many and such severe problems coming my way at the same time.

I was stuck in a limbo for many months. I was in London at the time; it was a pre-planned trip for my birthday. Maybe I was in the happy vacation-mentality or maybe I was just too far away to know how much worse things had become. But while I was there, I kept thinking, *"We'll be able to manage this."* When I got back to India, actually saw what was going on, and started meeting with investors, I realized the gravity of the situation.

And that triggered a very bad phase for me. Just thinking about what all had happened, what all I needed to do, and the fact that I did not really know how to reverse that unfortunate situation made me very anxious. I was physically and mentally drained, I had started getting palpitations, and I had started feeling like a loser.

Eventually, the worst thing that I had fought so hard to avoid during the years of Covid happened- we had no money to pay salaries. And I thought that would be the end of my journey. Along with the crushing pain and disappointment that I felt for myself, I did not want this for my team. They deserved much better.

Just as I thought everything was collapsing, Utsav called me one day with the news that we had got some money from a client. That would give us a runway of about 2 months. At that moment, all I could think was that this was a sign from above.

God himself had decided that it was not time for our story to finish, so how could I even think of letting it finish?

That's when I took a deep breath, steadied myself, and decided to go back to the basics.

I started cutting down on costs. I wanted and needed to cut down on almost 90% of the costs, and naturally, this could not be done overnight. It had to be approached gradually. Almost 2 years were taken up by this endeavor. I started back in 2022 and finally, now in 2024 is when we're managed to bring down the costs in the proportion and manner that we wanted to.

But this was only one part of the action plan to revive and thrive the business. Parallelly, we needed to find ways to increase revenue and profitability. We needed to make the company sustainable enough that it would never again run out of reserves. But this was extremely difficult given that we were not able to secure funding.

I knew that we could not achieve any of this without a strong and motivated team. And so, keeping up the morale of our people became another important addition on our to-do list. I needed to fuel that spark again in them, inspire them to put their heart and soul into their work, and give them the confidence that we were surely going to overcome that low. This was a slow and steady journey, and this too took almost 2 years.

It's so ironic when I think back about the root cause of all this. What was the instigating factor that actually caused this domino fall? Of course, there was nothing we could have done about the government's rule to ban the game. But our problems had truly started much before that and we had invited them in with our own hands.

That first and very sweet taste of success had slightly derailed us. At a time when we should have worked even harder, we ended up slacking. We let ourselves get too comfortable (something that entrepreneurs can never afford to do) and that turned out to be our undoing. And I would say this is the most important lesson I've learned through all the years that I have been working.

You can never afford to lose sight of what you want to achieve, especially not after you've taken a few successful steps toward achieving it.

A lot of things have happened in the 2 years since this phase. We managed to cut our costs while scaling our profits. We still face a lot of rejections and the market is in a rather bad shape.

But I've come to realize one thing. Giving up is not an option that I can, or want to consider.

I had not started the company with the intention of getting famous or rich (though I am extremely grateful for the popularity and financial security that it has brought me).

I started it with the intention of proving to myself that, *"OMG...I can do it!"* The choices that you make when you feel like you are running out of options defines who you really are. And usually, the right choices are always the toughest ones! And I wanted to make that right choice and follow through with it till the end.

The company is like my baby and however bad things got, I could never get up on it. That was the driving force that kept me going through all the hardships. To date, this is the one thing that I always keep in mind.

Along with this, I kept thinking that an 'underdog' like me had been given this chance to be a part of something so good and be the founder of a funded company. If I let it go, the chance may not come my way again.

And the last thing I wanted people to think was that I had got everything by fluke. That I had just got lucky, or been in the right place at the right time. That would not only have undermined all the hard work that I and my team had done, but it would have given a very wrong message. Where I hoped to inspire others who felt as I did at one point of time, I would have just made them believe that an underdog could not really achieve things.

So, I chose to keep fighting against anything and everything that would come our way. We take it one week, then one month, then one quarter, and then one year at a time.

Securing funds, acquiring customers, cutting costs are, no doubt, extremely important for us. But, we have our priorities set so that even if these things are not happening at any point of time, we have to keep going. We have to keep making choices (that may be tough sometimes) and sacrifices for what we have set out to create.

And this mentality is extremely important for an entrepreneur, sometimes even more important than the resources, vision, skill, or talents that you may have. It's ultimately going to be you (and if you're lucky, your team will stand with you) against the world.

This was something I learned the hard way, I hope that my experiences and learnings can help someone else. During that challenging time, there were a few people from whom I expected help. They started giving me cold responses. Blowing me off without really being honest enough to say so. It was all about how "I would get out of this" or that "The times would change" or that "Every business goes through ups and downs".

The clear subtext behind all these was that we cannot help you and that I was not good enough.

Worse still was the unsolicited advice that came my way. I was repeatedly told to just quit, give up, and let go if I cannot manage things. I can now safely turn a deaf ear to these, but back, it would often confuse me whether there was any merit to these suggestions that I was getting. It was also rather hurtful.

But I thank my stars that I never paid too much heed to it! Because it's what made me realize that no problem is big enough to crumble my will.

Chapter 10

"The woods are lovely dark and deep but I have promises to keep and miles to go before I sleep"

- Robert Frost

Without even perhaps realizing it, we have come very far together, have we not?

Baring my heart and soul on the pages of this book, I have made you all my confidantes for some of the best and worst memories and experiences of my life. You know every version of me that has ever existed, right from the backbencher to the businessman. You know my trials and triumphs.

And now, I want to unfold yet another, but a very significant facet of my life. Circumstances, no doubt, have played a pivotal role in making me what I am today.

But along with those circumstances, there is something else that has contributed to it. To be more specific, there is someone. And to be even more specific, there are many such 'someones'.

Like a potter gently uses his hands to mould the clay and delicately uses his fingers to give it the crevices and curves that we see, these people have played a similar role in my life. They have changed the way I see and assess the world. And no story of mine can be complete without them and without sharing all the immeasurable ways that they impacted my life.

If you're thinking this is a chapter about parents, siblings, spouses, or friends, you are only partially right. These people have undoubtedly guided me, supported me, and even healed me with their love, wisdom, and patience. But some of the instances that I will be sharing here are from people who I never really knew well and who are not even a part of my life today.

I have come to believe that I was destined to meet them in each of those specific scenarios, because they were the channels through which I had to gain some crucial learnings. Or perhaps, it was simply a wild twist of fate.

Whatever be the reason, these people, the experiences (both good and bad) that I had with them, and the things they taught me are a big part of my journey.

It seems rather unimaginable for one person to essay so many roles, right? My brother, Harish Goel, was born into only one of these roles. Not only did he fulfill that in the most exemplary way possible, but he slipped into these other roles too over the course of our relationship.

The ten-year age gap between us made him almost like a father figure to me. There has never been a day when I have not felt inspired by him, nor has there been a day when he has not tried to seek the best for me.

In fact, I remember he was the one who instilled some semblance of studiousness in me back in my early school days, when I would study the bare minimum to just pass and claim the gifts that he would promise me for my results!

When my parents and I first went to visit the college in Dehradun from where I went on to do my graduation, I was very underwhelmed. I was already unhappy about not having any other prospects, and when I saw the building, that feeling escalated.

It was small and simple; nothing like the grand campuses I had seen in movies and nothing like the impressive colleges that my brother had studied from. That night, when I spoke to him on the phone, I had fully prepared a speech about why that college was not meant for me and how I should try my luck in Delhi instead.

After hearing my grumbles, he said to me, "Don't look at the size of the college. Look at the size of the opportunities you are getting. You may be feeling that you're starting at a point behind where your friends from IIM and other top colleges at are.

But remember, you will meet them again someday and there will be a level playing field from there onwards. So really, all that matters is how good you are and how hard you're working for what you want."

That advice has never left me, and it has really changed how I think about challenging situations. Whenever I'm interacting with someone, I have stopped thinking about how big, famous, or qualified they are, and instead think only about what I can do better. Because he opened my eyes to the things that really matter.

He made me realize that a strong head start can only get you to a point, because that's where everyone else starts catching up to you. And there onwards, the only thing that determines whether you make it or not is your grit and resilience.

What I am about to share is a story about something that happened to me when I was barely 13-14 years old. But you can imagine how important it was because I remember every detail of it to date.

There was a very popular drink during those days called *Banta Soda*. I too used to love it, and I would often go to a shop to drink it. It used to be priced for 3 rupees 50 paise, and I often used to leave from home with 4 rupees in hand. The shopkeeper used to routinely not give me the change with the simple logic of, "It's just 50 paise! It's not a big deal!"

Not only had I somewhere started agreeing with him, but it also gave me a sense of having an upper hand that I was leaving behind tips to him. This went on for several months till one day, I went with a friend to that shop. I was short of around 2 rupees and I confidently gave him my remaining money and told him that the balance could be settled later. That look of disdain on his face, and the way in which he said, "If you don't have the money, why have you come to buy it at all?" shook me up.

As I got into the business world, I kept that lesson close to me and told myself that nobody is really out there to be your friend. You may have done numerous favours to other people, but the day you ask for a favour, you're looked down upon. Especially when it's a monetary favor. I felt extremely insulted that day and it probably wired me to hate the feeling of being in debt or having to ask anyone for money.

The other important lesson that I learned highlighted a big mistake that I had made. I had been, unthinkingly, giving away so much money. Looking back, I don't think that the shopkeeper was wrong in not wanting to excuse me for that payment of 2 rupees. He was just running his business. I was wrong for not being more mindful, and getting caught up in how 'cool' it made me look. I have vowed never again to repeat such mistakes.One of the most important lessons I learned was when I realized I had made a big mistake, something I hadn't really known till this point, so I just stepped back and reflected. It was careless to the degree that I had been virtually throwing money around like it was a game or a way of trying to prove some sort of point. I remember the moment clearly—when the shopkeeper refused to let me off the hook for just 2 rupees. At first, I thought it was unfair, but looking back, I see it differently. The shopkeeper was simply running his business, as he should. It wasn't about the 2 rupees; it was about the larger picture. I had become so enthralled with the idea of giving money out and getting this "cool" feeling, as if I were above all the ordinary problems people face. But the reality was that I was unconscionable and irresponsible. I simply lost my sense in the fantasies of a person I was not.

In that moment, I realized how wrong I had been. It wasn't about showing off to anyone, it wasn't about the fleeting sense of superiority-it was about paying attention to what I was doing and the impact it would have on life. I strongly felt a sense of remorse at never valuing what I had and being so out of touch with people. So from that day onward, I vowed never to commit that blunder again. It was not just about money; it was about knowing the real effect of my decisions, making sure I never got lost in the sham of trying to appear something I was not again.

After I completed my graduation, the years between 2005 to 2007 were spent in a limbo. I had not taken my final year too seriously, and consequently, I did not have any options of good colleges for an

MBA. I also needed money for it; money that I knew we did not have.

I did not want to burden my brother any more than I already had, and my father did not have any savings at that time. This is not one of my proudest moments, but I want to lay it all out there- I started blaming my father for my condition.

I started thinking that if he had worked harder and made more money, I would not be in that boat. Unfortunately, these thoughts sometimes even made their way into my interactions with him, something that I will forever regret. Once, when I was frustrated about not getting a job, I lashed out at him for it. I felt terrible about it for days, but I could not really undo it.

This is something almost each of us is guilty of doing at some point or another. We place unfair blame on other people and try to use them as a means to escape facing our own shortcomings. But if my work has taught me anything, it is to always take ownership for your mistakes. If you excuse yourself from the guilt of it, you will naturally excuse yourself from the onus of fixing it too.

And that will get you nowhere in life. Also, if you think about it, most of the problems or difficulties that we think have come our way have actually been brought there by us. We are responsible for what we do, and hence, what good can possibly come from blaming someone else for it?

If there's any possible way that I could get my hands on a time machine, I would wind it back to that day when I said these things to my father and instead, tell him all the wonderful things for which I have him, and only him, to thank. He has given me the calmness, patience, and composure that has got me out of many tight situations. Where others would perhaps lose their cool and let everything blow up, he taught me how to remain grounded and keep things together.

Before I found my path toward my MBA, I had taken up a job as a door-to-door salesman. The job itself was fine, and I was actually quite good at it too. What was not fine (at all) was my attitude. I had become bitter and self-pitying; a combination that can almost never produce any positive results.

I had to travel by bus for it- something that crores of people do every day- but I felt very ashamed about it. I would act like I was sneaking around to do something wrong, would often get off at a bus stop far from the office, just to ensure that nobody knew the truth of how I was getting there. I kept thinking about how others could afford cars and drivers while I was being forced to use public transport, and this contributed to the bubbling mixture of negative emotions in my mind. I had barely worked for 10 days when it just started getting too much.

I broke down in front of my mom. As any mother would do, she gave me the confidence that I desperately needed and told me that I should leave it and wait till something better came my way. Powered by her pep talk, I went up to my boss. But even there, I just could not hold back my tears. I told him about how I wanted to pursue an MBA but did not have the money for it. And again, all this was because I was coming from a place of feeling sorry for myself.

My boss tried to calm me down and then, he whispered something in my ear. "Don't pity yourself."

Over the years, I have added some more nuances to this valuable advice he gave me. Though I could not understand those unsaid words, what he was truly trying to tell me (and the message that I am trying to pass on to others) is that, "When you pity yourself, you're degrading yourself. You're making yourself out to be helpless when, really, you are not. And you're also giving the world an invitation to see you like that."

This advice, though very significant, is not at all easy to adopt. When things get really tough, the most comforting option sometimes is to just feel bad for yourself. But that simple statement was so powerful that it has steered me clear from choosing this option in many difficult situations. I firmly tell myself that with self-pity, I am lowering my own value.

Back in my MBA days, there was a senior professor who was one of the most calm and composed people ever. He used to teach a rather boring subject, which never really made sense to me. He became the target of many of the jokes and mean comments that are typical for college students to pass, both to his face and behind his back. However, I never once saw him get angry or irritated about this. He was extremely knowledgeable and he would focus all his efforts on trying to spread that knowledge.

In one such instance, where a student was fooling around and trying to make a joke of the professor, he imparted a very important message. He told the student, “I know you’re not serious about your education because it clearly shows. The kind of outlook and attitude you adopt is how people are going to see you too. And that sticks on. It becomes the image that people have of you.”

The professor, as I mentioned, rarely ever reacted or said anything in retaliation. But when he did, he ended up teaching me something that was more important than any college syllabus.

Before that day, I had never realized just how significant the impact of my attitude would be. If I did not get serious in my mind about things, that attitude of mine would get broadcast to the world through my words or actions.

I would be sending a signal that I’m not serious, and conveying the message that I am not someone who can be relied upon to get things done, simply because I can never take things seriously. And this mostly stays with you forever.

That’s when I learned about the kind of outlook that I needed to develop in life. Whatever I was doing, I needed to do it seriously and sincerely, giving it my 100%. The way that I portrayed myself to the world was very important because it was the basis on which people would evaluate me.

After that day, I never cracked another joke against him. I realized that I did not want to be seen as a jokester who found his amusement at the expense of other people. And the first step to ensuring this was to stop presenting myself as one.

So, from then on, I made sure that I did not act like a joker during my college days. I knew I needed to change, not for others, but for my own growth. I realized how easily humor at someone else's expense could diminish my worth as a person, and I didn't want to be known as someone who only entertained others by putting them down. I wanted to be taken seriously, to be respected for who I truly was, not just for the laughter I could provoke.

As I stepped away from this habit, I realized that my way of interaction began to change with others. No longer was it necessary to make a joke in order to gain people's attention; hence, I realized people were relating with me in a more authentic way. I felt more valued, and it felt rewarding to know that I wasn't just the guy who could make others laugh, but someone who had substance. It was a shift I didn't expect to feel so deeply, but it was one I was glad I made.

The source of yet another eye-opening lesson for me was also one of my college professors. He taught us business communication and soft skills, and his classes used to be so engaging that I genuinely enjoyed attending them. Not only was he a very handsome and well-dressed person, but he carried himself wonderfully. I used to try to copy this, especially his fluent and confident way of speaking in English.

He had this one philosophy that he had told us about, and which changed the way I went about life.

The difference between where you are today and where you will be after 5 years is determined by 2 things.

First, by the kind of things you read, because you assimilate whatever you read and it shapes your mindset. It gives you not only knowledge, but it broadens your perspective. I also picked up many autobiographies on the way. Reading about people who had overcome struggles, achieved great things, and made their mark in the world gave me direction. Their stories offered me lessons that I could apply to my life. Besides the books, this change in attitude also helped me connect with others on a deeper level. I found it easier to network and engage with people who could offer guidance and open doors for me by presenting myself as someone who was to be taken seriously. I started receiving valuable insights and opportunities that I might not have had access to before. This was the sort of growth that I was longing for, and I learned that personal change had much to do with how people perceive one's self in addition to one's self-image. Second, by the kind of people that you associate with, because you adopt the kind of qualities that you see often in others. So, being around people who are insincere or have no drive to succeed will make you the same. Instead, you can choose to be around sincere, hardworking, or motivated people and have these qualities eventually develop in you too.

If you think about it, they are such simple things that we can easily control. But they have the potential to change the trajectory of our life. And I have held on to that philosophy to date.

I try to read as much as I can. And I try to ensure that whatever I am reading contributes to my life in some way. I try to read books related to my field of work, about self-help, or the inspiring stories of people who have already done what I aspire to do someday in my life.

I also try to interact as much as I can with such people. I did not realize it back then, but somewhere along the way, the positive and inspiring influence of my siblings and parents must have rubbed off on me and shaped my actions and decisions!

Saurav Patnaik, as you may now know, played a major role in the development of my life's story. Working under him at Kenscio was a turning point for me. There's quite an interesting story about how I got there in the first place. Though I was going in for an interview, I did not have a strong base of marketing expertise. But that's not what he asked me at all. Instead, he asked me general questions, probably to just test my communication skills and to see how I composed myself.

And I'm so grateful that he took a bet on me based on that interaction.

I was always amazed by his aura; the way he walked, talked, and dressed. I never felt like just an employee working under him. I always felt like an equal, like-minded businessman, because he always interacted with me like that. And the more I talked to him, the more I began seeing myself too in that light.

During one such interaction, he told me, "If you want to learn how to communicate better, see the styles of some other people who are good at it and just copy them. And from this, you can create your own style."

As was the case with everything that he told me, I took this also very seriously and started blindly copying people. Be it actors, businessmen, or any other famous personality, I picked up whatever traits I liked from many people and tried to use the same in the way I spoke, dressed, or acted in public. I also adopted a lot of things from Saurav himself!

Eventually, as he had predicted, I ended up creating a unique style for myself. It was an extremely valuable piece of advice, because it showed me the way ahead when I was confused about how to start communicating better. In fact, I too have passed on this advice to anyone who reminds me of the place that I was once in, in the hopes that they too can benefit from it as much as I did.

He contributed a lot in giving me the confidence and skills that are needed in setting up a business. Whatever I may do in life or wherever I may find myself, the time I spent with him and the things I learned from him will always remain close to me.

The role of an investor is typically thought of only in terms of putting down money into a business. However, I feel lucky to have found some people who not only did this, but also left me with very important and significant learnings.

Mr. Sharan Parikh is an investor in our company, but I have to regard him as an elder brother. There has never been a time when I have met him and not marveled at the kindness and warmth he possesses. He is someone with whom I can not only discuss my business, but even expose my vulnerabilities.

In times when I have felt stuck, overwhelmed, or just unsure of what I needed to do, he has always been there to guide me. When the company was going through one of the toughest times it has faced and we were struggling to raise money, I told him one day that I just could not do it anymore. I felt like I was being personally rejected by potential investors and started wondering whether there was really any fault with me.

"You're too hard on yourself!" is what he told me. "You're the one who's struggling, putting in money and so much effort, just to keep the company alive. Think of yourself as a fund manager, and you will realize that you're doing such a good job. You're laying low when it is needed and you're looking to scale when it is needed. As a fund manager, you're doing exactly what you should be and not letting the company collapse."

For the first time, I started thinking about myself and my role in a different way. I truly was managing the funds of my investors and trying to grow them. If I had just quit, I was not only putting myself in a position of loss but I was doing the same for them too.

When he told me that he admired the maturity with which I was handling everything. It really boosted my confidence. It made me see what my real purpose was, and how much I had actually done, instead of only focussing on the things that were slipping out of my control. This change in perspective was just the thing that I needed to keep me going.

Vikrant Varshney, Managing Partner - SucSEED Indovation GROWTH Fund, is another such person. There is immense mutual respect and regard in our bond, which is why it holds such a meaningful place in my life.

I have always been sure of the fact that I never want to sugarcoat things for my investors. Whatever be the situation, I want to always present them with the complete truth. During a very low period in our business, around July- August of 2022, our runway had been exhausted and I did not know whether the business would even sustain till the next month. It was heartbreaking, but I put all this down in an email and sent it as a part of the monthly updates that I provide to investors.

A lot of the recipients simply gave me no response. A few of them asked me about what we had in mind and what our plan of action was. But, his was the only response that really stood out. He said that he appreciated my honesty; appreciated the fact that as a founder, I had come clean about the extremely challenging state of my business.

He praised a quality in me that, till then, I had not even thought of as something praiseworthy. The decision to never mislead my investors had just come very naturally to me, without having put in much deliberation toward it. But he made me see it as a strength. That single email fired up a spark in me. Even when all seemed lost, even when it seemed like we had not done well as founders, he was someone who believed in us and gave us the confidence that we were doing things right.

He gave us a lot of his valuable time and advice after that, and opportunities too that helped us turn that situation around. He made me believe in myself again, and his words of encouragement meant the world to us.

“Founders are like artists,” he once said to me. “You start with an open canvas and start building art. You may have a vision of what you think the completed picture will be, but when you finish it, it might look different. It will still be a beautiful picture, however. You just have to expand your imagination and see it in that way."

This was such a wonderful analogy that it has always stuck in my head. And whenever I feel that things are deviating from what I had planned, this keeps me grounded. Because I know that the end result, though different from what I had planned, will still be good.

Our funding journey started with SOSV (Orbit Startups). As I am talking about the role that great investors can play in an entrepreneur's life, I would be amiss to not mention it and in particular, Oscar, William, and Nick. They have supported us, encouraged us, believed in us, and been right there with us. They have always pushed us to do more and to get ourselves to the next level.

I once asked William about the right time to raise funds. He very simply told me, "You're always raising funds!" The message behind this was that as a founder, you simply have to keep hustling. The mythical time after a fundraise when you can just sit back and relax never really comes. Because the minute you step back, things can start taking a downward dip. Oscar is the one who gave me that golden advice about how money is best raised when you don't need it, because that's when you have the power to negotiate. Nick, as our portfolio manager, has seen the most difficult times of our careers and lent us a helping hand to get out of it.

I truly wish that every entrepreneur out there is blessed with investors like this. Because sometimes, that one kind word or one good gesture is the only hope that someone needs.

And with this, we come to an end. The end of this book, but surely not the end of my journey! I know there is a lot more left to achieve, and a lot of people whom I want to make proud.

I hope that my story has made everyone who ever felt an underdog believe that they too can do great things, only by being themselves and staying true to their dreams! I can personally vouch that it worked for me...

Verses Kindler Publication

Reach us through our website -
https://www.verseskindlerpublication.com/
For more information visit our Instagram or Facebook page.